Enlightenment
PRANAY

BUDDHA
WISDOM LIBRARY

Published by

FiNGERPRINT!
Prakash Books

Fingerprint Publishing
@FingerprintP
@fingerprintpublishingbooks
www.fingerprintpublishing.com

ISBN: 978 93 6214 556 7

Remembering our Buddha-nature
takes us rapidly toward enlightenment.

*May the light of wisdom illuminate your path,
May the river of compassion flow endlessly in
your heart, May the winds of peace carry away
all turbulence, May your journey be adorned
with serenity and joy.*
—**A Buddhist Benediction**

*One lamp can dissipate the accumulated
darkness of a thousand ages!*
—**Tilopa, the Great
Buddhist Master of Indian
and Tibetan Mahamudra**

*Wordly matters will carry on,
but don't delay meditation!*
—**Milarepa of Tibet**

Contents

CHAPTER 1

The Buddha's Way to Enlightenment

The very essence of Gautam Buddha's path is the pursuit of complete enlightenment (*mahabodhi*). Enlightenment, in the Buddhist sense, signifies the attainment of ultimate liberation and truth. The inspiration drawn from Buddha's pursuit of enlightenment has awakened millions of people throughout history, transcending eras and borders.

Gautam Buddha's message regarding enlightenment emphasizes the need for the mind to release its grip on concepts and attachments, thereby transcending the limitations imposed by the mind. Buddha's teachings guide us toward complete bravery, liberation, clarity, and an understanding of the inherent sanctity within existence. The essence of Buddhism lies in achieving absolute clarity of heart and mind—a quality that bestows us liberation, boundless joy, and courage like the Samurai!

Central to the Buddha's teachings on enlightenment is the imperative to break free from the cycle of birth, death, and rebirth. This is accomplished by embracing the Buddha's Four Noble Truths, which form the foundational principles of Buddhism. These truths entail understanding the nature of suffering, its causes, its cessation, and the path leading to its cessation. A clear comprehension of these aspects, as elaborated in subsequent pages of this book, guides us toward living an enlightened life.

The Buddha presents the Noble Eightfold Path as the means to progress toward enlightenment, consisting of:

1. Right understanding
2. Right intentions
3. Right speech
4. Right actions
5. Right livelihood
6. Right effort
7. Right mindfulness
8. Right meditation or concentration.

By focusing our awareness on the Buddha's transformative teachings, we undergo profound personal growth. We cultivate mindfulness and meditative practices, leading to profound clarity, inner peace, and progression toward enlightenment. In this process, we naturally develop compassion and become agents of positive change in the world, embodying true success.

The Buddha's path to enlightenment emphasizes benevolence toward oneself and all beings in the vast multiverse we share as fellow travelers.

Gautam Buddha's path to enlightenment provides clear guidance on attaining ultimate wisdom and awakening—known as *Bodhi* in the Buddha's language of Pali, *Wu* in old Chinese, and *Satori* in Japanese. The Buddha's attainment of perfect enlightenment is referred to as *Samma-Sambodhi*.

THE SEVEN FACTORS

The Seven Factors of Enlightenment (Satta Bojjhanga) are qualities the Buddha identified as essential for attaining enlightenment or Nirvana. These factors are:

1. Mindfulness (*Sati*): Being present and attentive to the current moment, observing phenomena without judgment or attachment.

2. Investigation of Phenomena (*Dhammavicaya*): Inquiring into the nature of reality with wisdom and discernment, examining phenomena deeply, and breaking free from delusions.

3. Energy (*Viriya*): Generating persistent effort and diligence in walking the Buddhist path, overcoming obstacles and negative qualities.

4. Rapture (*Piti*): Experiencing a sense of joy, happiness, and spiritual upliftment as one progresses, reinforcing commitment and motivation.

5. Tranquility (*Passaddhi*): Achieving a state of inner calm, peace, and composure, free from agitation and restlessness.

6. Concentration (*Samadhi*): Developing a one-point focus and unification of the mind, essential for deep insight and meditation.

7. Equanimity (*Upekkha*): Maintaining a balanced and impartial mind, free from biases and aversions, embracing all experiences with acceptance and serenity.

These seven are interdependent and support one another, forming a comprehensive path to enlightenment. By cultivating these qualities, one progressively purifies the mind, gains profound wisdom, and ultimately attains the cessation of suffering and the realization of Nirvana.

MINDFULNESS

Mindfulness plays a pivotal role in Buddhism's pursuit of enlightenment, advocating for consciousness to remain firmly rooted in the present moment, fostering profound calmness and undisturbed tranquility. This dedicated practice cultivates a more profound wisdom within us. The tripartite wisdom in Buddhism serves as a beacon, illuminating the path and dispelling the shadows of ignorance. It underscores the unwavering belief that regardless of life's circumstances, the journey toward enlightenment remains open to all—a testament to the boundless compassion inherent in the Buddha's teachings.

AWAKENING

In Buddhism, spiritual liberation, awakening, and enlightenment are denoted by the terms Nirvana or *Bodhi*, which imply a state marked by a profound understanding of reality and freedom from suffering. Delving into these foundational principles of Buddhism leads to a detachment from conditioned beliefs about grief and sorrow. Central to the Buddha's teachings on enlightenment is the realization of the true nature of reality, encapsulated by the concepts of impermanence (*Anicca*), suffering (*Dukkha*), and non-self (*Anatta*).

Embracing these principles empowers us to become more dynamic and attuned to the present moment, allowing us to awaken to our true nature. Establishing ourselves in the present moment is the veritable path toward enlightenment.

However, enlightenment isn't solely achieved through intellectual understanding; it necessitates cultivating wisdom, compassion, and adherence to a moral code. This multifaceted approach enables us to transcend ignorance, attachments, and delusions. As we progress toward enlightenment, we are rewarded with profound peace, freedom, and liberation—representing the ultimate aspirations of the Buddha's teachings.

CHAPTER 2

The Inner Buddha

I n Buddhist philosophy, "Buddha-element" or "Buddha-nature" refers to the inherent potential for enlightenment that exists within all sentient beings. It signifies that every living being possesses a pure, luminous essence akin to that of a fully enlightened Buddha. In other words, it implies that each individual has an inner seed of Buddhahood (the *Buddhadhātu*).

In a broad sense, Buddha-nature is considered an inner, intrinsic quality that already exists within, regardless of our current state of spiritual attainment. It is a dynamic potential that can be actualized through the cultivation of wisdom and compassion, ultimately leading to the realization of full enlightenment or Buddhahood.

A common metaphor used to illustrate Buddha-nature is that of the moon obscured by passing clouds. It represents the idea that while Buddha-nature is ever-present and luminous, it can be temporarily obscured by mental afflictions, such as greed, hatred, and delusion. However, just as the clouds eventually dissipate, revealing the moon's radiant presence, the removal of these defilements through spiritual practice allows one's innate Buddha-nature to shine forth, unveiling the true, eternal, and unchanging nature of consciousness.

Buddhism describes various kinds of awakening and enlightenment, such as *dunwu* or sudden awakening, and higher states like the perfect enlightenment of Buddhahood, known as *anuttara samyak sambodhi*. Recognition of the Buddha within awakens us to move toward perfect enlightenment.

Zen Buddhism takes this concept further, emphasizing that we should not *seek* our inner Buddha but *see* it as already present within us! Zen teaches that we are originally Buddhas who have simply not yet awakened to that fact. The path to complete enlightenment becomes most natural and spontaneous once we awaken to this realization of inner Buddhahood. The main aim is direct insight into one's true nature (for which meditation such as *Zazen* is also used).

Eventually, Zen encourages us to be in an easy and effortless flow, remaining natural amidst all circumstances and situations. This implies trusting the higher Buddha-nature within us and continually taking small steps on the journey toward enlightenment—regardless of the challenges we may face along the way! It is all eventually about having resilience (like the Buddha did on his path to enlightenment), accepting circumstances, and cultivating inner peace . . .

"Life is like carrying a heavy load over a long journey; don't rush. When you accept discomfort as normal, you will not feel discontent."

人生は重荷を負って遠き道を行くがごとし。急ぐべからず。不自由を常と思えば不足なし。

Tokugawa Ieyasu, the Japanese Shogun

CHAPTER 3

Tilopa's Teaching on Enlightened Living

Tilopa, the eminent Buddhist master of the Mahamudra ('Great Seal') Tantra of India and Tibet, imparted the most profound teaching for enlightenment, saying:

"Don't recall. Don't imagine. Don't think. Don't examine. Don't control. Rest."

This guidance is a crystal-clear lesson on embracing the enlightened meditative energy that is naturally joyous, spontaneous, and effortlessly dynamic.

It equips us to face life in a way that is enlightened, intuitive, insightful, courageous, clear, and swift, devoid of mental clutter. Tilopa's ancient instructions are for our liberation. His golden spiritual rules are intense and fiery, providing a path for navigating life's difficulties.

Under Tilopa's advice, the final instruction— "Rest"—does not mean inaction; rather, it involves cutting away unnecessary anxious thoughts and being anchored in one's highest state of a blissful, enlightened being.

By releasing the mind's fears completely, our consciousness and energy will become clear, enabling dynamic action. In this way, a spontaneous light illuminates the path to enlightenment . . .

CHAPTER 4

Zen Buddhism's Powerful Teachings for Enlightenment

From the withered tree,
A flower blooms.
A Haiku by Issa symbolizing
the universal potential for
renewal and sudden awakening

Ancient Japanese Zen Buddhism imparts some of the most direct, profound, practical, and empowering lessons for enlightenment and awakened living. Among the myriad teachings of Zen, several key lessons stand out:

1. Empty yourself of all preconditioned notions, allowing a fresh perspective to emerge.

2. Recognize that truth transcends the confines of the mind; question and discern without blindly accepting mental constructs.

3. Embrace relaxation amidst the ordinary activities of life, paving the way toward enlightenment through a serene and tranquil mind.

4. Master the art of silence to open the channels of the mind and heart, facilitating more profound understanding and connection.

5. Engage in choiceless awareness, remaining fully present and receptive to the unfolding of each moment as preparation for enlightenment. This spirit of *choiceless awareness* is at the very heart of Chan, Seon, and Zen Buddhism (the closely related teachings from China, Korea, and Japan, respectively).

6. Cultivate joy and lightness through smiling and laughter, easing the journey toward enlightenment.

7. Focus on the present moment, letting go of preconceived notions and embracing the immediacy of experience. Such immediacy is the crux of the Zen Haiku of mystic poets such as Basho, Dogen, Ikkyu, Ryokan, Issa, and others.

8. Release worries and anxieties, transcending them through mindfulness and inner peace.

9. Embrace the art of "not knowing," creating space within the mind for the illumination of enlightenment to arise.

10. Look inward to discover the light of enlightenment within oneself, recognizing that true enlightenment arises from self-awareness and inner transformation.

11. Cultivate a calm state of mind as a foundation for enlightenment, fostering clarity and insight.

12. Harness your emotions and channel them into graceful actions, infusing each moment with beauty and harmony.

13. Recognize that enlightenment transcends the confines of any specific path, religion,

or mental state, embracing universality and inclusivity. Such inclusivity and universality can be found in the mystical verse of several Buddhist poets—such as Wang Wei, Hanshan and Shide of China, as well as Jinul and Hyesim of Korea.

14. Embrace the inevitability of death without fear, understanding that enlightenment encompasses a balanced approach to life and death.

15. Embrace acceptance as a fundamental aspect of enlightened living, allowing for growth and transformation through openness and receptivity.

16. Prioritize what truly matters in life, disregarding distractions that hinder progress toward enlightenment.

17. Shift your focus toward asking meaningful questions rather than seeking to find all the answers, fostering curiosity and exploration exhaustively.

18. Embrace the mystery of existence with openness and wonder, recognizing that true enlightenment lies beyond comprehension.

19. Place trust in the Buddhas' wisdom and surrender to the vastness and interconnectedness of existence, relinquishing the ego's need for control. This is a key aspect of Thiền Buddhism, which is the Vietnamese form of Zen.

20. Harness the innate thirst for enlightened living as a driving force, propelling you on self-discovery and spiritual growth.

21. Dedicate your entire life to the pursuit of truth, recognizing that each moment offers an opportunity for profound insight and awakening.

22. Trust in your inherent wisdom and transcend doubt, courageously ascending the symbolic mountain of enlightenment.

23. Engage in meditation and attentive awareness of thoughts, fostering a bold awakening to the true nature of reality.

24. Let the purity of innocence guide you along the path to higher truth, embracing simplicity and authenticity in your spiritual journey.

25. Move beyond the limitations of words and scriptures, accessing a state of pure being that transcends intellectual understanding.

26. Approach mundane tasks with a spiritual mindset, bridging life's material and spiritual aspects to cultivate harmony and balance in all endeavors.

By integrating these teachings into our lives, we embark on a profound journey of self-discovery and spiritual growth, ultimately realizing the boundless potential for enlightenment within each of us.

CHAPTER 5

Buddha and Buddhism's Words for Enlightenment

Gautam Buddha has said several things which put us firmly on the path toward enlightenment. The myriad Buddhist scriptures contain powerful words to catalyze our transformation and quest for enlightenment. We must heed these messages! Some of the words personally spoken by Gautam Buddha and the Bodhisattvas are:

1. Do not dwell upon the past. Do not dream of the future. Instead, concentrate the mind on the present moment.

2. Hatred does not cease by hatred but only by love. This is the eternal law.

3. All we are is the result of what we have thought. The mind is everything, what we think we become.

4. Work out your salvation. Do not depend on others.

5. One word that brings peace is better than a thousand hollow words.

6. Rise and be thankful. If we didn't learn much today, at least we learned a little. And if we didn't learn a little, we didn't get unwell. And if we got unwell, at least we didn't die. So let us be grateful.

7. The secret of health for both consciousness and the body is not to mourn and worry about the future, not to worry about the past, not to anticipate things with worry, but to live in the present moment with earnest zeal and wisdom.

8. There is no path to happiness; happiness is the path!

9. You will not be punished for your anger. Your anger will punish you.

10. Peace comes from within. Do not seek it outside.

11. Three things cannot be long hidden. The sun, the moon, and the tree.

12. Just as a candle cannot burn without the flame, men cannot live without a mystical or spiritual life.

13. In the end, just three things matter. The quantum of how much you loved, how gently you lived, and how gracefully you let go of things that were never meant for you in the first place.

14. Do not overrate what you have received, and never be jealous of others. The one who is envious of others can never attain true peace of being.

15. Health is the greatest gift, contentment is the greatest wealth, and faithfulness is the best relationship.

16. Believe nothing, no matter where you heard it or read it or who said it, even if I have said

it, unless the thing agrees with your reason and sensibility.

18. The root of all suffering is attachment. Be detached.

19. A jug fills drop by drop. Be patient.

20. The tongue is like a sharp knife. It can kill and do violence without even drawing blood.

21. The mind is everything, what you think you become.

22. The only real failure in life is not being true to the best one knows and can be.

CHAPTER 6

The Seven Treasures

*Hidden in the mountains is a mysterious
market . . . There, you can barter the noise
of common life for endless light!*

Milarepa of Tibet

Buddha imparts teachings on the
seven riches or "treasures" that
guide us toward enlightenment.
These seven riches or treasures are:

1. Listening to the dharma attentively, emphasizing the importance of paying close attention to Buddhist teachings.
2. Cultivating great faith in the path.
3. Exercising great discipline in our actions and behavior.
4. Cultivating deep meditative practices.
5. Demonstrating true zeal and dedication to our tasks and spiritual practice.
6. Embracing renunciation, letting go of unnecessary attachments.
7. Upholding moral integrity, walking the path of ethical goodness.

CHAPTER 7

Buddha's Mystical Inspirations for Enlightenment

The Buddha's message is more about inner qualities than any rituals of religion. His vastness, simplicity, and profundity—all simultaneously—hold the ultimate mystic message for mankind. The attempt in this chapter is to condense the Buddha's most important teachings for enlightenment—in a format that is fresh, insightful, understandable, and accessible to all. The humble effort is to encapsulate the Buddha's timeless teachings in a way that can guide us in contemporary living. His message has the most profound significance for both the present and the future of mankind.

In other words, this chapter is a condensed version of Buddha's core mystic keys for readers globally. The objective of the following spiritual insights or principles has been to distill the essential depth of the Buddha's greatest teachings while keeping it simple . . .

WISDOM AND ENLIGHTENMENT

Wisdom and enlightenment come from self-contemplation.

BUDDHA-NATURE

The Buddha-nature is within all things: perceive the divine and become transformed and enlightened. The term "Buddha-nature" translates several Mahayana concepts, including *tathāgatagarbha* (womb or embryo of the "Thus-Gone One") and *buddhadhātu* (Buddha-realm or Buddha-element). This primordial, undefiled mind, the tathāgatagarbha, is often equated with the ultimate reality of emptiness (*śūnyatā*).

JOY
The greatest joy is finding the Infinite, deep within your inner self.

THE INNER BUDDHA
Within you is the timeless and enlightened witness of all things, your unshakeable inner Buddha.

EVOLUTION
Don't be too worried or self-concerned: this is key for your evolution toward enlightenment.

HOME
Your true home is the meditative space within, rest in it.

BUDDHISM
Real Buddhism means creating a meditative vibe within oneself and one's environment: it is beyond religion, race, ideology, or sect!

EXCELLENCE AND ENLIGHTENMENT

Allow the meditative attitude to become part of your life. This is the Buddha's secret to true excellence and enlightenment.

ENERGY

Do all things with the completeness of your energy: Buddha's mystic way to enlightenment.

PLAYFULNESS

Being playful and joyful in all things—work, relationships, meditation—is the mystic way of the enlightened *Boddhisattvas*.

WATCH YOURSELF

Watch yourself silently and peacefully: this is real meditation. This is the way of the *Arhats*.

POTENTIAL

Inner silence unlocks your purest potential.

PATIENCE

Khanti, or patience is the foundation of the Buddha's awareness.

RELAXATION

Being relaxed within is true meditation.

SPONTANEOUS HAPPINESS

Natural and spontaneous happiness is created through *karuna* or compassion.

COURAGE

The Samurai warrior's courage arises from the meditative space within: this is the key to being a real enlightened warrior.

PRAYER

Real prayer is internalization: going within, silently, into meditative trance.

FAITH

Faith, or *shraddha*, is the ability to put one's complete energy into the present task within the present moment.

MENTAL EQUILIBRIUM

Upekkha or mental equilibrium—having an equal attitude to all, without judgment—creates real happiness.

SELF-KNOWING

Self-knowing is the Buddha's teaching for creating inner brightness, inner radiance, and intelligence.

KINDNESS

Metta or kindness/friendliness is a natural by-product of the meditative attitude.

WELL-BEING

Mudita, taking joy in others' well-being is the secret to our well-being; never take pleasure in another's unhappiness.

MEDITATION

Jhana or meditation unlocks your highest inner strength and intelligence.

RELIGION

All the paraphernalia and show of religion are nothing if they miss the meditative soulfulness at the heart of the Buddha's message.

RADIATE NOBLENESS

Radiate your noblest qualities amidst all circumstances: the Buddha taught that inner nobleness or *'ariya'* is the highest human quality.

BUDDHA FOR TOUGH TIMES

Regardless of the situation, consciousness's power is always greater: always be optimistic, even during tough times.

DHAMMA

The *dhamma* or real teaching of the Buddhas is about going beyond thoughts and freeing the mind-heart-consciousness of all senses of limitation.

AHIMSA

Ahimsa, the real non-violent attitude, emerges through pure observation, without comparison, judgment, or prejudice.

KARMA

All material entities—from the individual microcosm to the cosmic macrocosm—are entwined through the law of *karmic* reciprocity.

FEEL LIMITLESS

Feel limitless by releasing the mind from conditioned thought.

INWARD RICHNESS

The greatest inward richness is our inexhaustible energy to share inner peace and bliss, should we choose to.

DISSOLVING ANXIETY

First, slow down, becoming serene and relaxed, and then watch as anxieties dissolve spontaneously.

EASE

Great ease floods your being when you're content to be alone.

CALM CONSCIOUSNESS

Meditation is an attitude of calm consciousness amidst all things, not a separate activity.

AFFECTION

Make affection or *sneha* your core inner quality, like breathing, instead of reserving it for certain people only.

BECOME NOTHING

Become nothing to become one with everything: leave the ego far behind.

BURN

Let anxious thoughts burn out and sublimate through the natural fire of your consciousness.

NIRVANA

There never was a time when you were not a Buddha: knowing this leads to awakening, taking you a step toward *nirvana* or liberation. Nirvana implies complete extinction (of suffering, etc).

TRUTH

When you negate all untruth, truth emerges on its own . . .

THE FORMLESS

Our reality is formless, beyond the forms of body and brain.

QUIETNESS

Even within the noise of the world, be quiet within your consciousness.

MAITRI

Looking at the world with a friendly eye or *maitri* (friendliness) generates waves of well-being within oneself: this is the law of the 'Maitreya Buddha' or future Buddha of Universal Friendliness.

THE TATHAGATHA

The *Tathagatha* (as Gautam Buddha used to refer to himself) taught the spirit of being inwardly tranquil, above all things.

EFFICIENCY

The meditative attitude creates efficiency in all our actions.

MINDFULNESS

True mindfulness happens through heartfulness.

THE SECRET

The secret or *gupt* teaching of the Buddhas is the effortless and relaxed inner state: like the effortless yet mighty flow of a river.

MAYA

Illusory attachment or *maya* takes us away from our essence and inner grandeur.

SILENCE

Silence is meditation.

BECOMING FREE

Compassion and love create real freedom and enhance the power of consciousness.

INSIGHT

Insight and intuition are your greatest allies, always available in inner quietness.

UPROOT

Uproot all thought about meditation while meditating, and be free!

BEING GUTSY

Both courage and love blossom when there is no 'I' or ego.

WORK ON SELF

The Buddhist attitude is simple: by working on ourselves, our work in the world too improves!

ABHAYA

The Buddha's *abhaya mudra*, or gesture for courage, is symbolic of placing the top-most priority on being fearless: all things flow from that state.

CHOICELESS AND PURE AWARENESS

Choiceless and pure awareness are greater than any 'system' of meditation or spiritual *sadhana* (practice).

DEFOCUS

Defocus from hurt and forgive all: this sets you free and generates happiness.

FORGET

To be free, forget the past, and negate the over-importance of emotional memory.

VANISHING

In real *jhana* or meditation, the meditator vanishes.

THE MYSTIC SEARCH

The mystic search means first dropping all religious authority and spiritual formulae.

SERVICE

The Buddhist foundation of service is first through the transformation of yourself.

BEYOND

Beyond body, mind, and feelings is the compassionate domain of Buddhahood.

GRATITUDE TO NATURE

Gratitude to nature creates a rhythm and energy of natural inner joy.

ONE DISCIPLINE

Buddha had one primary discipline for the *sangha*, his followers: remember the Buddha within you!

INSTANT CALM

Instant calm can be achieved by relaxing the breath: this is a simple key to the Buddha's way.

TIBETAN BUDDHISM

At the heart of Tibetan Tantrik Buddhism or Vajrayana is effortless meditation.

DANCE

Let your consciousness dance with delight, in gratitude to the Infinite.

REST

Rest in higher consciousness, silent and serene . . .

CREATING BLISS

Inward silence creates bliss.

JAPANESE BUDDHISM

At the heart of ancient Japanese Buddhism was an insistence on transforming each physical activity into a meditation.

SPIRITUAL BEAUTY

The ancient Indic and Buddhist symbol of the lotus signifies that we can ascend to spiritual beauty even while existing within worldly circumstances.

TRANSFORM

The Buddha transforms a single moment into an eternal one . . .

ANXIOUS THOUGHTS

Anxious thoughts imprison us in limitations: drop them now.

THE FIRST STEP

The first step toward Buddhahood is seeing the spiritual vastness that is already within you.

AWAKENING INNER JOY

The meditative attitude doesn't really *produce* joy; it simply helps awaken the inherent spiritual joy that is already within you.

INSTANT PEACE

Instant peace comes through discarding constant thoughts.

WITHIN

Creating quietness and a relaxed attitude within yourself leads to strength, peace, true success, and happiness.

MATURITY

Maturity implies being in control of thoughts and not letting thoughts control you.

CLARITY

Buddhism is primarily about achieving such clarity that one can perceive the divine element within one's being.

THE MISTAKE

Schools of meditation often make the mistake of lulling the practitioner into dull and overly relaxed states, while real Buddhist meditation is about awakening to *bodhi*, or higher consciousness.

TRUE BRILLIANCE

True brilliance is revealed through discarding unnecessary thoughts, which move like clouds upon the clear sky of consciousness.

KNOWING

Knowing one's being as *chetana* or pure consciousness is Buddhism in essence.

ALL ARE SPIRITUAL

Buddhism's greatest gift to the world is the assertion that there are no spiritual or unspiritual beings: all are as capable of being Buddhas!

WITHIN

The mystic Buddha-nature moves deep within you, a constant current of energy.

DETERMINATION

Siddartha Gautam Buddha's life is a testimony to the power of determination for realizing all things mystical.

TREASURE

The luminous treasure of your Buddha-nature awaits your decision to seek it.

MAKING WAY

Body-consciousness and mind-consciousness must make way for the realization of pure consciousness.

MYSTIC ENERGY

Cultivate your mystic energy.

WASTE

All pursuits are a waste without meditative energy.

BE COOL

Be cool within, remembering that your being is made of the pure light of *satti* or awareness.

DON'T TRY AND CONTROL EVERYTHING

Surrender is often the way to flow with fresh energy: we cannot control everything.

TANTRA

In *tantra*, sexual energy represents our fundamental enlightenment—energy, like a ripple on the lake or a wave upon the sea.

TENSION

Tension is the pull between past and future; relax about both.

DON'T BE AFRAID

Never be afraid of what may happen; through being vulnerable, we develop divine vision, become rooted and strong in truth itself!

NO EXACT ANSWERS

There are no exact and ultimate answers, only good questions.

REAL RICHNESS

The Buddha's bliss and enlightenment are God-like, yet they are attainable for us as well.

HOPE AND HAPPINESS

Hope and happiness begin with auto-suggestion: as you believe, so you become!

DIVINE ENERGY

All things arise out of divine energy and dissolve back into it; what is there to worry about?

IT CAN'T BE TAUGHT

The true way of the Buddhas cannot be taught or learned, but only experienced.

WINNING

The only way to truly "win" in life is through higher awareness: it is the way of the Buddhas.

PATIENCE AND PEACE

Khanti (patience) creates *shanti* (peace).

TRULY REALIZED ONES

The truly realized ones know that being a "thinker" confined to the constraints of the "mind", is never enough to know cosmic truth and vastness!

ENRICHMENT

Real enrichment—and real empowerment—begin with imbibing the mystic vibe.

PERFECTION

There cannot be anything close to perfection in material terms, but enlightenment is close to perfect in mystic terms.

BUDDHIST OR BUDDHA?

Gautam Buddha didn't want his disciples to *remain* just Buddhists but *to become enlightened Buddhas*!

LOGIC IS LIMITED

Logic is limited, reason is limited, and mysticism is unlimited.

GRACE

The Buddhas—and true Buddhists—bring grace to each action, each word, each gesture.

GOD-LIKE

The Buddha's bliss and enlightenment are God-like, yet it is possible for us to attain them too.

THE GREATEST TEACHING

The Buddha's greatest teaching is that we are already Buddhas.

> *In the space between thoughts,*
> *wisdom shines bright!*
>
> Milarepa, the Great
> Tantric Yogi of Tibet

CHAPTER 8

The Divine Is an Inner Experience

Contrary to many religions that conceive of the divine as an external, supernatural entity and creator, Buddhism presents a unique perspective—the divine is an inner experience. Buddhism asserts *the inner Buddha*.

In Buddhism, the divine is not an object or an external being; instead, it is seen as an experiential reality within oneself. According to Buddhism, true godliness is to be personally experienced, not merely *believed* or based on theological writing or dogma.

Buddhism asserts that the supreme energy resides within each individual, and one can come to know this divine essence within oneself without relying on external belief systems or the existence of an outer God. The journey involves observing oneself from within, leading to understanding the innermost divineness and a state of being beyond anxiety. The superconsciousness that can overflow within an individual depends on how deeply rooted one is within oneself.

From a Buddhist perspective, life is an opportunity to delve deep into the roots of the divine that exist within. Instead of glorifying an external God or deity, Buddhism exalts the individual and emphasizes the innermost search. It is fundamentally meditative, focusing on exploring one's inner being rather than seeking an external God.

The core teaching is to look beyond the ego, thoughts, and conditioned mind to discover the energy beneath—an energy that constitutes one's innermost core. Within this energy resides the bliss of the divine, making the divine itself an inherent part of one's being. Buddhism, thus, invites individuals to embark on a journey of self-discovery and inner realization, recognizing the divine as an inner experience that transcends external manifestations.

BUDDHISM: INNER COMMUNICATION WITH THE DIVINE

Buddhism advocates a unique form of communication with the highest possibility, transcending traditional concepts of prayer or communication with an externalized God. This form of communication is profoundly internal, requiring individuals to explore and connect with something within themselves that surpasses the limitations of the mind and extends beyond the reach of thoughts. Buddhism, therefore, carries a sense of great dignity, asserting that within each person lies something more expansive and significant than the mind can comprehend.

From the Buddhist perspective, discovering this inner essence leads to a life of creativity, true wellness, and healthfulness. It propels individuals to reach the peaks of their being, unveiling their highest reality. This highest reality, known as the Buddha within, is considered a reflection of the divine. Buddhism does not advocate the need to seek an external divineness or objectified God. Furthermore, concepts of hell or heaven are viewed as internal states rather than external realities. In the absence of an objective God, hell and heaven become internal states that individuals can create within themselves. However, Buddhism acknowledges that these states are illusory, as beyond them lies the blissful Buddha state—the state of pure being and pure consciousness within the inner cave of one's being.

Buddhism emphasizes an inner effort, an intense introspective journey wherein miracles and bliss unfold. The ultimate goal is to go deep into the inner cave of consciousness, meditating in the profound silence and peace within, eliminating the need for external settings like caves or mountaintops. The summit of the mountain is found within, in the depths of inner peace and tranquility.

BUDDHISM: INNER EXPERIENCE

In Buddhism, the divine is not viewed as a commodity acquired through external means such as prayer. Instead, the divine is seen as an experience lived through individual meditation. The essence of Buddhism lies in the understanding that inner freedom is paramount, challenging the notion of being bound by an external power. It asserts that the real treasure and inner splendor are inherently within, waiting to be discovered through personal choice.

While external monasteries may provide a material environment and a vibration of calmness, Buddhism emphasizes that the true importance lies in the monastery of one's innermost heart. Over time, Buddhism, like other religions, may have become entangled in rituals and regulations. However, these external aspects serve the fundamental purpose—a meditative exploration of inner divineness and the discovery of the inner God.

The emphasis is not on getting entangled in outer rituals and purifications but on non-resistance within the inner being. Non-resistance allows individuals to delve deeper into the beautiful and profound aspects of the self. The search for God is fulfilled when approached with an open heart and an open mind, realizing that one is a medium for the pure consciousness—the Buddha—within. Allowing this inner divinity to surface turns individuals into instruments of their inner divinity, embracing spontaneity. In this realization, the perceived distance between oneself and the divine dissolves. It becomes an illusion, and one attains a profound peace of mind through this understanding. Ultimately, Buddhism leads individuals to this core of peace, making it a central aspect of the philosophy.

THE INNER ESSENCE OF LIGHT AND PURITY

Buddhism emphasizes that within each individual resides the great light of purity, akin to the highest heaven. The teaching encourages seekers to embark on an inner journey to discover these inherent qualities. This is more important than seeking answers through external means or praying to an outer being. According to Buddhism, the real listener exists within—the deep inner silence, the purity of consciousness.

Unlike the dilemma of questioning the existence of God on the outside, Buddhism directs individuals to explore within. The philosophy dismisses the need to grapple with external inquiries about God's presence and how to approach Him. According to Buddha, all one needs to discover can be found inward. The answers are not dependent on priests, theological books, or religious philosophies. Instead, real communion with the inner self is essential in spirituality and mysticism.

Buddhism is a path to uncover the foundation of bliss, freedom, godliness, and the divine within one's being. The focus is on the inner journey, and the teachings emphasize the profound connection between the individual and the intrinsic qualities that lead to the realization of godliness. The deities in Tibetan Buddhism such as the Medicine Buddha, Jhambhala, Phalden Lhamo, and Mahakal remind us to find the divine potentiality residing within ourselves!

CHAPTER 9

Teachings from the Yogachara School of Buddhism

On the path toward enlightenment, the Yogachara School of Buddhism teaches us several things. First, it tells us about those *wholesome mental attitudes* that we must inculcate within us to truly quicken our progress toward enlightenment.

These attitudes are:

1. Faith (*shraddha* in Sanskrit and *dad pa* in Tibetan).

2. Decency (*hri* in Sanskrit and *ngo tsha shes pa* in Tibetan).

3. Modesty (*apatrapya* in Sanskrit and *khrel yod pa* in Tibetan).

4. Lack of craving (*alobha* in Sanskrit and *ma chags pa* in Tibetan).

5. Lack of ill-will toward others (*advesha* in Sanskrit and *zhe sdang med pa* in Tibetan).

6. Lack of delusion (*amoha* in Sanskrit and *gti mug med pa* in Tibetan).

7. Energetic vigor (*virya* in Sanskrit and *brtson 'grus* in Tibetan).

8. Calmness, serenity, and tranquility (*prashrabdhi* in Sanskrit and *shin tu sbyangs pa* in Tibetan).

9. Vigilance, wakefulness, and alertness (*apramada* in Sanskrit and *bag yod pa* in Tibetan).

10. Equanimity (*upeksha* in Sanskrit and *btang snyoms* in Tibetan).

11. Complete absence of harmful intentions toward others (*avihimsa* in Sanskrit and *rnam par mi 'tshe ba* in Tibetan).

Furthermore, the Yogachara School of Buddhism elucidates the afflictions hindering progress toward enlightenment. These afflictions are categorized as the *root afflictions* (called *mulaklesha* in Indian Buddhism and *genben fannao* in Chinese Buddhism) and the secondary afflictions (called *upaklesha* in Indian Buddhism and *sui fannao* in Chinese Buddhism). In the Vajrayana Buddhism of Tibet, the root afflictions are referred to as *rtsa nyon*, and the secondary afflictions as *nye nyon*.

The afflictions to be avoided include over-excessive lust or sensuality, known as *Raga*; anger, termed as *Pratigha* or *Krodha*; ignorance, labeled *Avidya*; pride, identified as *Maana*; skeptical doubt, named *Vichikitsa*; and wrongful views, called *Drishti*. Additionally, the afflictions to steer clear of are resentfulness leading to anger or resentment (*Upanaha*), maliciousness (*Pradasha*), hypocrisy (*Mraksha*), deception (*Maya*), deceit (*Shathya*), arrogance (*Mada*), hostility (*Vihimsa*), jealousy (*Eershya*), a selfish attitude (*Matsarya*), indecency (*Ahrikya*), lack of modesty (*Anapatrapya*), lack of faith (*Ashraddhya*), weariness of energy (*Kaushidya*), heedlessness (*Pramada*), sloth (*Styana*), restlessness (*Auddhatya*), forgetfulness of our true nature and ultimate reality (*Mushitasmritita*), lack of caution (*Asamprajanya*), distraction (*Vikshepa*), drowsiness (*Middha*), over-worrying (*Kaukrtya*), being fixated in our thoughts (*Vitarka*), and continual thoughts upon objects (*Vichara*).

CHAPTER 10

The Power of Silence

SILENCE:
THE ESSENCE OF CREATION

Buddhism asserts that everything resides within silence (*mounam*). It is the profound foundation of both us and the cosmos. Silence is the origin of prayer, peace, and spiritual understanding—a state of meditativeness.

SILENCE IN BUDDHIST SEARCH

The core of Buddhism lies in silence. Embracing, absorbing, and recalling the silence within is the path to the divine. It guides the transition from thoughts to the heart, despair to hope, dullness to dynamism, and beyond.

FULFILLMENT THROUGH SILENT REALIZATION

According to Buddhism, true fulfillment comes from silent realization. This contribution of the Buddha emphasizes the eloquence of silence, expressing the highest truths, gratitude, and eternal awareness. Words are limited, but silence is boundless.

BUDDHISM'S EMPHASIS ON SILENCE

Buddhism strongly emphasizes silence over prayer. Examples can be found in Zen Buddhism in Japan and meditative Buddhism in Southeast Asia. Silence becomes a rare and invaluable quality in a world saturated with constant chatter, both globally and individually.

SILENCE AS THE CREATIVE ESSENCE

Behind all words lies a profoundly creative space shaping the cosmos. At its deepest level, this essence is silence. Falling into silence brings us back to the original divine state, the source of all valuable things. The greatest phenomena emerge from the silent state of the divine, where God's whisper is heard in the beauty of creation.

RICHNESS FOUND IN SILENCE

Silence is both the path and destination for the heart, offering the fragrance of life. Essential qualities like courage, hope, understanding, and awareness are rekindled in silence. Like the silence in soil nurturing a seed, meditative states activate and gather energy for the journey ahead.

SILENCE AS CORRECTIVE ABILITY

Silent meditative states are considered the most corrective ability for humans. Gautam Buddha exemplified and emphasized this discipline, not only for monks but also for lay followers. Meditative silence brings one closer to the ultimate heartbeat, allowing the gathering of energies without the burden of words.

KNOWLEDGE AND
SELF-CORRECTION IN SILENCE

From a mystical perspective, loading the mind with excessive knowledge is futile. True correction happens within the self-silence of the mind. This creates a sense of blessing, gratitude, and being on the right path. Silence becomes the discipline through which individuals move toward unity with themselves, free from conditioned thoughts.

REALIZING BLISS
THROUGH SILENCE

The essence of Buddhism lies in realizing your song of bliss, a universal and meaningful journey containing the fragrance of Buddha Himself. The sublime path of Buddhism focuses on realizing bliss through silence, as opposed to prayer, which can sometimes dull the mind with its repetitive patterns and conditioned responses.

SPIRITUAL AND MYSTICAL QUALITY BEYOND WORDS

True spiritual and mystical qualities cannot be cultivated through words dominating and overpowering our self-nature. Liberation from the grip of words is a challenging quest in the modern age. Creating the feeling of silence brings humility, and courage arises in liberating oneself from words. This quest requires patience, a sense of waiting, and a deep receptivity to life's mysteries.

OPENNESS TO LIFE'S IMMENSE MYSTERY

Buddhism emphasizes activating the innermost core and all dimensions within oneself, moving beyond conditioned beliefs. According to Buddhism, living intelligently is synonymous with living silently. Expressiveness should be powerful when needed, but silence allows the spontaneous gathering of energy, enabling a joyful and energy-filled response when the moment demands. Buddhism encourages living through the heart with empathy and compassion, activating the innermost core.

SILENCING THE
INNER DIALOGUE

In Buddhism, the inner dialogue is seen as a drain on energy, causing anxiety about various aspects of life. The spontaneous spiritual act is to move beyond this inner dialogue, being less concerned about the confusion created by words. Breaking free from the circle of words reveals glimpses of real freedom, Nirvana, or salvation.

POWER IN SILENCE

A silent person becomes powerful, as reflected in the Samurai's way in Japan. Influenced by Buddhism, the Samurai realized their potential in silent moments before battles. They would write death poems in total inner silence, channeling their inner dialogue into a few words. This process created a conscious and subconscious silence, connecting them with the divine, their deepest energy, and a sense of inner freedom. Letting go of useless thoughts and focusing on the task through silent internalization is encouraged.

HARNESSING SILENCE FOR INNER POWER

Silence as a stepping stone to passionate and dynamic moments is key to living optimally. To summon maximum inner power, it's crucial to stop leaking energy through unnecessary words and endless internal dialogue. Buddhism suggests a rhythm between silence and expressiveness. The silent person gathers energy to speak, when necessary, from a clean and innocent space, embodying a purity of relaxed courage.

THE VALLEY AND PEAK OF SILENCE

In Buddhism, the cycle of our states of inner consciousness is likened to peaks and valleys: undulating, fluctuating up and down. Silence is found when retreating into the 'valley' of the self. Resting in this valley allows one to climb the metaphorical mountain with renewed vigor the next day. The principle emphasizes a balanced approach between silence and expression, acknowledging that speaking up is important but more impactful when words originate from a clean, innocent space.

THE EAGLE AND THE PARROT

Drawing upon a Buddhist metaphor, the state of inner quietness is likened to an eagle that flies silently in the high portions of the sky, soaring upon winds. This is contrasted with a parrot, chattering endlessly but unable to reach great heights. To ascend to mystical heights, the mind must shed artificiality and its obsession with words. The natural state centers oneself in the purity of consciousness, accessible through the beauty of silence.

UNVEILING INDIVIDUALITY
THROUGH SILENCE

Engaging in constant arguments and chatter often doesn't enhance intellect; instead, it may lead to a dulling effect. The intellect tends to echo conditioned thoughts and ideas gathered from external sources. True individuality surfaces when one delves deeper, finding moments of peaceful, silent, meditative solitude. Inner aloneness involves nurturing the hidden flame of energy, shining brightest when attuned to the silent cosmic music of divine energy. This connection facilitates realizing one's multi-dimensional potential, fostering a synthesis of mind, body, heart, and soul. Silence, in its subtlety, emerges as a potent force for genuine success.

CHAPTER 11

Exploring Our Buddha-nature

The profound concept of Buddha-nature, or Buddha-Dhatu, illuminates the pure essence within each individual—a core that transcends layers of personality, national identity, and religious affiliations. Nestled deep at the heart of the self, it is a field of pure listening, seeing, and being. Buddhism views everything as transient, but the Buddha-nature, the field of bliss, stands beyond material boundaries.

The journey in Buddhism is a continuous rediscovery of this Buddha-Nature, leading to the oneness of being and the integration of inner selves. Realizing this state grants a sense of perfect ease and authority, where the perfectly balanced watcher and listener reside, inseparable from the whole.

In this state, circumstances and responsibilities no longer disturb; instead, there is a liberating feeling of being in command of one's being. The capability to shoulder necessary responsibilities emerges effortlessly. Buddhism identifies man's tendency to dominate due to ignorance of his Buddha-nature. The realization dawns that there is nothing to dominate, for deep within, one is already fulfilled.

Entering this inner realm satisfies all thirst, making material desires seem insignificant. The importance shifts to the nature of oneself, where perfect intelligence is found, and non-separateness with the cosmic melody is realized. Rediscovering one's Buddha-Nature becomes the ultimate spiritual victory—a realization that one is a true winner, never to be defeated in the realm of spiritual fulfillment.

BUDDHA-NATURE: AWAKENING THE VICTORIOUS FLOW OF INNER BEING

In the material world, victory and loss prevail, but one stands eternally victorious within the field of the Buddhas. This wisdom is the key to emerging as a true individual, allowing the natural flow of one's being to surface from the deepest realms. The practical value lies in the alchemical and transformative nature of this awakening—an inner revelation that brings relaxation, a sense of self in harmony with the world, and heightened effectiveness in thoughts, actions, and motives.

To experience the greatest aspects of life, one must tap into their innate Buddha-nature and let it permeate all endeavors. The awareness of beings is akin to an onion's layers: we too possess layers, conscious and unconscious, with suppressed emotions and thoughts. Beneath it all lies a clear listener and visionary capable of grasping cosmic truths and realizing the beauty and power within. In this state, misery becomes obsolete, and the manufactured thoughts of the mind are no longer necessary.

The Buddha-nature is characterized by utter simplicity, spontaneity, and fulfillment, surpassing any outer satisfaction. Represented by the lotus in Buddhism . . . it blooms even amidst unclean surroundings and muddy water! The symbolic thousand-petal Lotus signifies that Buddha-nature can shine through any circumstances, allowing individuals to be their most radiant, courageous, and unblemished selves. Deep within, a divine element transcends all limited circumstances—a metaphor for understanding that one can radiate one's true essence amid any situation.

ILLUMINATING DIVINE CONSCIOUSNESS IN EVERYDAY LIFE

The Buddha-Nature is synonymous with our divine consciousness, representing the culmination of life's evolution toward expressing this divine essence in our actions, emotions, words, and behavior. It is about transforming our very presence and conquering life's challenges by addressing the root cause—our bewilderment, anxiety, and fear of the material world. Rediscovering and bringing forth the Buddha-nature from within us is the key to a palpable and transformative presence that transcends inner anxieties.

To come close to our Buddha-nature, the path involves becoming more meditative in all dimensions, emptying the mind's content, and recognizing the enlightenment already within us. While humans often function based on pleasure and pain, the Buddha-Nature is in perfect balance, not compelled to chase or avoid either. It can exist peacefully amid pleasure and pain, embodying gratitude, grace, and strength.

Realizing our inner Buddha-nature is described as a lightning bolt in the middle of the night—an illuminating flash that can brighten the whole land, even if only briefly. The symbolism of lightning, found in various mystic traditions worldwide, represents the Thunderbolt of Indra, Thor, Zeus, or Jupiter. Just a small spark of recognition within oneself can illuminate the inner world and enrich inner life. When inner life is illumined, outer actions become infused with joy, rejoicing, and a sense of totality in energy.

TRANSFORMATIVE REALIZATION FOR INNER HARMONY AND COURAGEOUS LIVING

With its abundance of pleasures, the realm of the gods is considered less fortunate in Buddhism, making the infinite energy that transcends causality and circumstances—the innermost core. A profound non-tension and blissfulness emerge in this deep non-causal unity with the universe. This realization transforms individuals from the inside out, bringing meaning and unburdening anxieties.

While not everyone may reach ultimate enlightenment or nirvana, glimpsing the higher nature within is crucial on the path of Buddhism. The awareness that a high state of being is inherent within us frees us from anxieties, instilling a sense of inner freedom and courage. This courage propels individuals toward vaster paths, fostering hope and the realization of miracles in life. The magic of life unfolds in multiple dimensions, breaking the monotony of material pursuits.

Moving toward Buddha-Nature means recognizing a great light of being beneath layers of personality, nationality, and religion—a foundational part of oneself. This realization opens the door to inner freedom, harmony, and optimum functioning. The Buddha emphasizes that the human body is a perfect means to realize Buddha-Nature, as it experiences both sorrow and joy. With its abundance of pleasure, Buddhism considers the realm of the gods less fortunate, making the infinite openings of truth more accessible to human beings.

BUDDHA-NATURE: THE UNIVERSAL IDENTITY BEYOND MASKS AND MISERY

In Buddhist mythology, even the gods bowed down to the Buddha upon his enlightenment, acknowledging that he transcended their state of being. This act symbolizes realizing a higher state—our original identity—the essential field of Buddha-Nature. This identity goes beyond the masks we wear in the material world, such as those tied to dogmatism/fanaticism within society, nations, or religions. Dogma is, in Buddhism, identified as source of human misery.

Discovering Buddha-Nature involves disentangling oneself from material circumstances and becoming a perfect observer of life, seeing with an equal eye of wisdom and hearing the cosmic harmony. This journey leads to bliss, creating a mystical coolness and a non-disturbed, non-anxious state of being.

Knowing one's Buddha-nature means being non-perturbed, recognizing the liveliness of life in all dimensions, and connecting with the core mystical element that exists eternally. The energy of Buddha-Nature is readily available if one delves deeply enough—that is all that is essentially needed.

UNVEILING THE CREATIVE SPACE FOR ULTIMATE BLISS AND WHOLENESS

Buddhist meditation revolves around looking and hearing deeply, a practice to touch the originality within us—the creative space known as Buddha-nature. This space holds the potential for ultimate bliss and is where our true wholeness emerges. It is a latent expanse within, waiting to be unearthed and requiring only exploration.

From the Buddha's perspective, life's ultimate concern is to find meaning. The consciousness—the Buddha-nature—within each individual embodies that very meaning. It bestows everything needed for life, offering liberation and infusing various aspects of life, including relationships and work, with dynamism. Buddhism, therefore, holds practical value by illuminating even mundane aspects of life with the light of the greater. The realization of Buddha-nature enables individuals to be wholehearted, daring, and intelligent in their pursuits, guiding them in the proper direction.

CHAPTER 12

Four Lessons for Enlightened Living

ANATTÁ

Anattá, meaning "not-self" or "egolessness," is a key concept for enlightenment in Buddhism. It tells us that nothing endures, and there is no permanent "self."

Buddhism says nothing is permanent; all is a flux. All things come and go. There is no self, i.e., it can be called a not-self. Contemplating not-self (*anattánupassaná*) is a transformative practice leading to emptiness liberation (*suññatá-vimokkha*), with wisdom (*paññindriya*) playing a central role. Progressing through insights, from Dhamma-devotee to vision-attainer, and finally, to holiness, individuals become 'liberated by wisdom' (*paññá-muta*). The finality is enlightenment.

The *Anattá-Lakkhana Sutta*, or "discourse on the characteristic of not-self," has been key to enlightening myriad Buddhas over the eons.

IMPERMANENCE: *ANICCA*

The Buddha said, "Impermanence of things is the rising, passing, and changing of things, or the disappearance of things that have become or arisen. The meaning is that these things never persist in the same way, but that they are vanishing, dissolving from moment to moment . . ."

This is the teaching of *anicca* or impermanence, the key to our enlightenment.

Buddhism says we must understand one thing: all things are passing, transient, and impermanent. Once you understand this, you can strive toward serious contemplation and meditation to reach enlightenment, and not before. The Buddha says, "Whatever is subject to origination is subject to cessation . . . All manifest forms disappear. Strive earnestly!"

TRANSFORMING SHOCKS INTO ENLIGHTENMENT: A LESSON FROM SIDDHARTHA

Certain experiences can deeply shake us to our core in life. Siddhartha, later known as Gautam Buddha, encountered the sights of an old man, a sick person, a corpse being carried to cremation, and a monk in meditation beneath a tree.

These sights are known in Buddhism as the "Four Signs," which jolted him out of his normal state of consciousness and set him on the quest for enlightenment.

The lesson is this:

It is up to us to utilize the unexpected or shocking moments in life. We can either let these moments make us negative. Or spur us on to realizing our higher self-potential.

In the Buddha's case, he embraced the mystic path rather than ignoring or being broken by these shocks. Siddhartha utilized these profound experiences to search for truth, demonstrating the transformative power of facing life's realities with sensitivity and a quest for enlightenment.

Gautam Buddha and many of us respond differently to life's challenging sights. While some may become indifferent or discouraged, Buddha's example encourages us to use life's shocks as catalysts for growth.

His profound lesson is to find a higher purpose with unwavering determination, doing whatever it takes to discover our enlightenment. By embracing this approach, we move toward enlightenment, true excellence, and fulfillment in life.

BUDDHA'S MEDITATION FOR ENLIGHTENMENT

The Buddha had a special enlightenment meditation, called *alokasanna,* which he explained to his beloved disciple Maudgalyayana.

This meditation is about perceiving the mind as full of light. Imagine that the mind is illumined with brightness like daylight. This clears and unclouds the mind, perceived as suffused with clear, luminous light. This meditation is said to make you full of inner brightness.

It is believed to help you develop the Divine Eye, referred to as an *abhinna* in Buddhism.

Like this meditation, Gautam Buddha used various means to instruct individual monks and the *Sangha*.

CHAPTER 13

Core Buddhist Texts and Teachings for Enlightenment

Buddhism is an ocean of wisdom. There are so many Buddhist scriptures which guide us toward enlightenment. These include the Pali Canon or the Tripitaka, the oldest body of Buddhist canonical texts. The Pali Canon consists of three baskets, as it were. The

Vinaya Pitika, which are the rules for monastic discipline; the Sutta Pitika, which are the discourses of the Buddha; and the Abhidhamma Pitaka, the philosophical and consciousness-based analysis. The second kind of scriptures are the Mahayana Sutras, including the Diamond Sutra, the Heart Sutra, the Lotus Sutra, and others.

Mahayana Buddhism teaches that the potential for enlightenment is universal and places great emphasis on compassion.

The third type of scripture is the Tibetan Canon, which includes the *Kangyur*, the translated words of the Buddha, and the *Tengyur*, which are the commentaries by Tibetan and Indian scholars.

Apart from these, Buddhism has numerous texts in various languages, such as Japanese, Chinese, etc. All these scriptures eventually point toward the primacy of enlightenment as the goal of all human beings, particularly humans. Within the core Buddhist scriptures, we find the teachings for enlightenment, the primary ones of which are the Four Noble Truths.

The Four Noble Truths are:

1. The principle of acknowledging the existence of suffering.

2. Identify the cause of suffering in attachment.
3. Recognizing that all suffering can end.
4. The Eightfold Path is the means to end all suffering.

The Eightfold Path comprises:
1. Right View is understanding the nature of existence as it is in reality.
2. Right Intention, which means the cultivation of ethics and positive intentions.
3. Right Speech means speaking the truth and avoiding harmful speech.
4. Right Action, doing action which is non-harmful and ethical.
5. Right Livelihood and earning a living align with Buddhist ethics and key principles.
6. Right Effort, cultivating positive qualities.
7. Right Mindfulness, which implies developing present-moment awareness.
8. Right Concentration means focusing, meditating, and cultivating the right mentality.

These principles of the Eightfold Path lead to correct mental and emotional development and tell us how to achieve enlightenment in all its aspects.

In addition to the core teachings of Buddhism, several other fundamental principles guide practitioners toward enlightened living. These include the recognition of the three universal characteristics: *anicca* (impermanence), which reminds us of the transient nature of all phenomena; *dukkha* (suffering), highlighting the inherent dissatisfaction in conditioned existence; and *anatta* (non-self), emphasizing the absence of an unchanging soul or self.

Furthermore, the 'Middle Way,' central to Buddha's teachings, advises against extremes and advocates for a balanced, moderate approach to life. By cultivating moderation, practitioners develop the mental and emotional discipline necessary for the meditative path toward enlightenment.

Ultimately, these teachings culminate in the concept of *metta*, or loving-kindness, which encourages compassion toward oneself and all beings. By integrating these diverse teachings into their lives, individuals pursue ethical living and wisdom and cultivate the qualities essential for meditation and, ultimately, attaining *Nibbana* or ultimate enlightenment.

CHAPTER 14

Aspects of the Buddha

Understanding the various aspects and qualities of the Buddha is paramount for those aspiring to follow his path of enlightenment. His virtues serve as guiding principles for inner transformation and spiritual growth. On our path, we must seek to learn from the qualities, virtues, and myriad aspects of the Buddha. Here are his key qualities and multi-faceted aspects, condensed into ten simple descriptions about him:

1. He is revered as the awakened one, embodying the pinnacle of spiritual realization and enlightenment.

2. The Buddha's enlightenment, or bodhi, is a beacon of human serenity, offering inspiration for attaining inner peace and clarity.

3. Many of his teachings are conveyed in silence, inviting introspection and inner reflection to internalize profound truths.

4. Compassion flows through the Buddha's actions and teachings, epitomizing his path of kindness and empathy toward all beings.

5. The metaphor of the lotus blooming within our hearts symbolizes each individual's inherent truth and wisdom, encouraging introspection and self-discovery.

6. Nirvana represents the culmination of the Buddha's journey toward enlightenment and liberation from suffering, signifying complete freedom and transcendence.

7. The Buddha's teachings transcend worldly boundaries and limitations, resonating across

cultures, races, and generations, imparting timeless wisdom and insight.

8. Enlightenment unfolds within the stillness of the mind, emphasizing the importance of inner silence and contemplation.

9. Seeking the Buddha's grace involves walking the path of righteousness and compassion, aligning one's actions with his teachings.

10. Zen Buddhism emphasizes harmony and freedom, inviting individuals to seize each moment as an opportunity for awakening and self-realization.

THE TRANQUIL POWER OF THE BUDDHA

We must draw inspiration from the Buddha's tranquil demeanor and the tales of his enlightenment. Indeed, embracing moments of tranquility unveils profound insights and serenity. Cultivate inner stillness to transcend conditioned thoughts and access silent illumination. By emulating the Buddha's sacred grace, you can encounter his spirit within yourself. The journey to enlightenment begins with inner peace, serenity, and silence.

The Buddha's mastery transcends intellectual understanding; it stems from boundless compassion, profound illumination, and harmony with all beings. Follow in his footsteps by cultivating inner tranquillity and awakening higher wisdom. Understanding the Buddha requires transcending the confines of the mind and listening to the whispers of the heart. By doing so, you'll experience the Buddha's presence resonating within you, filling you with blissful illumination.

His teachings emphasize the importance of tranquillity, rooted in the lotus consciousness that blooms within each of us.

Mind is like the sky:
do not over-conceptualize and cloud it!

Marpa, the Great
Tibetan Tantric Yogi

CHAPTER 15

Mantras and Prayers

Buddhists around the world recite these prayers and verses as a means of nurturing virtues essential for enlightenment, compassion, and mindfulness in their everyday existence:

INDIA AND NEPAL

Pali: In the annals of Pali Buddhism, a ubiquitous mantra echoes through the ages:

Namo Tassa Bhagavato Arahato Sammā-Sambuddhassa. Its essence, a solemn homage rendered unto the Blessed One, the Worthy One, the Fully Enlightened One, resonates across monasteries and hearts. This sacred incantation, intoned fervently in the ancient tongue, serves as an emblem of veneration, a humble supplication for the Buddha's benediction and enlightenment's guiding light.

Sanskrit: In the annals of Sanskrit Buddhist liturgy, the revered incantation *"Gate Gate Pāragate Pārasaṃgate Bodhi Svāhā."* Emerging from the venerable Heart Sutra, this mantra bears the weighty significance of "Gone, gone, gone beyond, gone completely beyond, enlightenment, hail!" Its recitation serves as a conduit to summon the virtues of sagacity and enlightenment, aspiring to transcend the tribulations of earthly existence.

TIBET

In Tibetan Buddhism, the *Om Mani Padme Hum* mantra stands as a beacon of significance, revered as an invocation for enlightenment. Though diverging from traditional prayer, it holds sway as a potent mantra believed to encapsulate the very essence of the Buddha's teachings. The syllables "Om Mani

Padme" resonate with the spirit of compassion, while "Hum" embodies wisdom's profound essence. The rhythmic recitation of this mantra is esteemed for its capacity to cleanse the soul of negative karma, foster compassion, and illuminate the path to enlightenment. Linked intimately with Avalokiteshvara, the bodhisattva of compassion, it is venerated as the quintessence of compassion and wisdom. Its utterance serves as a conduit for invoking blessings, nurturing compassion, and purging the vestiges of negative karma.

JAPAN

Nam Myoho Renge Kyo emerges as a sacred mantra within the folds of Nichiren Buddhism, purportedly encapsulating the very essence of the Lotus Sutra. It is revered for its purported ability to guide practitioners toward enlightenment and surmount adversities, and its influence is deemed profound.

In the realm of Zen Buddhism, the "Heart Sutra," or *Prajñāpāramitā Hṛdaya Sūtra*, holds a position of reverence. Its recitation serves as a conduit for delving deeper into the fabric of reality, unraveling its intricacies. Emphasizing the concepts of emptiness and interconnectedness, it offers a path toward enlightenment and relief from worldly suffering. An excerpt from the Heart Sutra, presented in both Japanese *Kanji* and English translation, exemplifies its essence: Japanese (*Kanji*): 観自在菩薩　行深般若波羅蜜多時照見五蘊皆空度一切苦厄 English: *Kanzeon Bosatsu* (*Avalokiteshvara Bodhisattva*), when practicing deep *Prajna Paramita*, clearly saw that all five aggregates are empty and thus relieved all suffering. This sutra elucidates the profound notions of emptiness (*śūnyatā*) and the interconnectedness pervading all existence, core tenets of Zen philosophy. Through the rhythmic chanting of this sutra, adherents seek to sharpen their perception of reality and inch closer to the elusive realm of enlightenment.

CAMBODIA

In Cambodian Buddhism, the oft-repeated prayers are:

1. *Namo Buddhaya* (homage to the Buddha)
2. *Namo Dharmaya* (homage to the Dharma)
3. *Namo Sanghaya* (homage to the Sangha)

SRI LANKA

In Sinhala Buddhism, the *Buddham Sharanam Gacchami* mantra resonates widely (it is part of the 'Three Refuges' mystic formula, or *Tisarana*). Its translation, "I take refuge in the Buddha," encapsulates a profound act of homage to the enlightened one. Recited fervently, it serves as a testament of devotion, a humble entreaty for the Buddha's benevolent guidance and sheltering embrace.

CHINA AND TAIWAN

Mandarin Prayers

In the tapestry of Chinese Buddhism, the mantra 南无阿弥陀佛 (pronounced *Namo Amituofo* in Mandarin) assumes a prominent place. Its translation, "Homage to Amitabha Buddha," embodies a profound act of veneration. Recited with reverence, it serves as an invocation for the blessings of Amitabha Buddha, beseeching entry into his Pure Land. This recitation, emblematic of Pure Land Buddhism, reflects the devout aspiration for rebirth within the serene realm of enlightenment.

In the realm of Chinese Buddhism, the mantra 觀世音菩薩 (pronounced *Guānshìyīn Púsà* in Mandarin) emerges as a notable presence. Its translation, *Avalokitesvara Bodhisattva*, resonates with profound significance. Devotedly chanted, it invokes Avalokitesvara (Guanyin in Mandarin), the embodiment of compassion. Through its invocation, practitioners seek to cultivate compassion within themselves and request blessings for personal enlightenment and the welfare of all sentient beings.

Chan Prayers

In the realm of Chan Buddhism, the focus often shifts toward silent contemplation, koan study, and dharma talks rather than the mechanical recital of specific mantras. However, within this contemplative tradition emerges an occasional invocation: the 心經 (pronounced *Xīn Jīng* in Mandarin), referred to as the "Heart Sutra." While it strays from the conventional definition of a mantra necessitating repetitive chanting, the teachings enshrined within the Heart Sutra wield immense significance within Chan discipline (as do the Diamond Sutra and Lankavatara Sutra). Practitioners, ensconced in the silence of meditation, may pore over the verses of this profound scripture, extracting profound insights to illuminate their spiritual odyssey. The ultimate goal is not so much scriptural as it is about having direct insight into the true nature if one's being!

Cantonese Prayers

In the Buddhism of the Cantonese-speaking people (particularly those who follow Pure Land Buddhism), a frequently heard mantra is 南無阿彌陀佛 (pronounced *Nàhmòu Āmeihtòuhfú* in Cantonese), which translates to *Namo Amitabha Buddha* in English. This sacred utterance serves as a gesture of reverence toward Amitabha Buddha, embodying profound devotion and mindfulness. Chanted devoutly, it is believed to evoke the refuge and blessings of Amitabha Buddha, guiding practitioners along their spiritual path toward enlightenment.

THAILAND

In Thai Buddhism, the widely embraced mantra นะโมพุทธานะโมทัสสะนะโมธัมมา (Homage to the Buddha, Homage to Him the Blessed One, Homage to the Dhamma), resonates with profound significance. Reverently intoned, it is a symbolic tribute to the 'Triple Gem': the *Buddha*, the *Dhamma* (teachings), and the *Sangha* (monastic community). Through its recitation, practitioners express unwavering reverence and devotion toward these foundational pillars of Buddhist practice and spiritual life.

KOREA

In the realm of Korean Buddhism, the mantra 南無阿彌陀佛 (pronounced Namu Amita Bul) holds a prominent position. Translating to "Homage to Amitabha Buddha," its utterance reverberates as a testament of devout reverence and unwavering devotion within Korean Buddhist circles. Recited fervently, it serves as a profound expression of veneration toward Amitabha Buddha, epitomizing the core ethos of Korean Buddhist practice.

MONGOLIA

The mantra Мөнх ялгуусны шүтээн (*Munkh yalguusnii shuteen*) weaves its significance into the tapestry of Mongolian Buddhism. Often transcribed as Өм маани бадмэ хум (Homage to the Buddha, Homage to Him the Blessed One, Homage to the Dhamma) in Mongolian Cyrillic script, it is the Mongolian pronunciation of the familiar "*Om mani padme hum*" mantra. This sacred invocation serves as a conduit for invoking the blessings of compassion and wisdom while also undertaking the arduous task of purifying negative karma. Its rhythmic recitation embodies the devout pursuit of enlightenment and the relentless quest for spiritual purification within the Mongolian Buddhist tradition.

VIETNAM

In the landscape of Vietnamese Buddhism, the mantra Nam Mô A Di Đà Phật echoes with profound significance. Revered widely, it serves as a conduit for paying homage to Amitabha Buddha, embodying the essence of reverence and unwavering devotion. Regularly recited within Vietnamese Buddhist circles, this sacred invocation punctuates meditation practices and daily devotions, symbolizing a heartfelt dedication to Amitabha Buddha's teachings and enlightenment.

This mantra, which is the Vietnamese pronunciation of the Chinese "Nāmó Āmítuófó" (南無阿彌陀佛), is indeed widely used in Vietnamese Buddhism, particularly in the Pure Land tradition.

MYANMAR/BURMA

In the realm of Burmese Buddhism, the mantra *Buddho Buddho* is a common refrain. Serving as a symbolic invocation of the Buddha's title, its recitation resonates deeply within the Burmese Buddhist community. Frequented in meditation sessions, this mantra becomes a vehicle for nurturing mindfulness and fostering profound reverence for the Buddha's example and teachings.

In Myanmar, reciting Buddhist mantras is a prevalent aspect of spiritual devotion. Among these, the mantra *Na Ma Hla* serves as a direct invocation to the Buddha. Additionally, the mantra *Chaw Thame Loke Thone* is frequently employed as a gesture of reverence toward the Triple Gem. These mantras, integral to the daily practice of Buddhist adherents in Myanmar, embody a solemn homage to the core tenets of their faith, reflecting a deeply ingrained spiritual tradition.

LAOS

In the realm of ancient Laotian Buddhism and Theravada Buddhism in general, the "Namaskara" or "Namaskara Gatha" is recited to pay homage and reverence to the Buddha:

Namo Tassa Bhagavato Arahato Sammā Sambuddhassa (repeated three times)

It means, "I pay homage to the Blessed One, the Worthy One, the Perfectly Self-Awakened One"

It is broken down as:

Namo - "I pay homage"

Tassa Bhagavato - "to the Blessed One" (Bhagavato refers to the Buddha)

Arahato - "the Worthy One" or "Accomplished One". It recalls the Buddha's enlightened state.

Sammā Sambuddhassa - "perfectly self-enlightened." Refers to the Buddha's perfect awakening

Such chants are a testament of reverence and homage to the Buddha, embodying the core principles of faith and devotion. Moreover, they serve as an earnest plea for blessings and safeguarding. These mantras, integral to the spiritual fabric of Buddhist practice, encapsulate the essence of veneration and supplication, echoing through the rituals of the sangha and the faithful.

INDONESIA AND SOUTHEAST ASIA IN GENERAL

In Indonesian Buddhism, the mantra *Namo Buddhaya* resonates as a familiar refrain. It is a solemn homage to the Buddha, embodying deep reverence and unwavering devotion. Regularly woven into meditation sessions and daily devotions, this sacred incantation epitomizes the devout reverence of Indonesian Buddhists toward the enlightened one, illuminating the path of spiritual enlightenment within the daily fabric of their lives.

BHUTAN

Akin to Tibetan Buddhism, a frequently employed Bhutanese Buddhist mantra is ༀ་མ་ཎི་པདྨེ་ ཧཱུྃ (pronounced *Om Mani Padme Hum*), echoing its widespread use in diverse Buddhist customs. Linked to *Avalokiteshvara*, the bodhisattva embodying compassion, this mantra reverberates to summon compassion, wisdom, and spiritual metamorphosis through its chanting.

CHAPTER 16

J. Krishnamurti and the Buddha

The mystic J. Krishnamurti's profound insights and vision reflect the deepest principles of Buddhism while remaining uniquely original. Krishnamurti was deeply influenced by the Buddha, even expressing that he would have sat at his feet if he had lived during the Buddha's time. Yet, he avoids the jargon of traditional religion, making his message of hope and inner power particularly relevant in the 21st century and beyond. Tirelessly traveling the world until an advanced age, his teachings have profoundly influenced figures like Bruce Lee, Aldous Huxley, and millions of others. His lessons are an updated version of Buddha's key principles for enlightened living.

Krishnamurti's teachings are imbued with Buddhist principles and aim to strengthen individuals from within, urging them to tap into their reservoirs of insight and perception to live an enlightened, strength-filled, inwardly rich, yet sensitive life. As a true world teacher, Krishnamurti's message of discovering one's inner courage and vision, even during the toughest times, reflects the essence of the Buddha's words.

It is important to remember that J. Krishnamurti was identified as the 'world teacher' at a young age. The prominent Theosophists Annie Besant and Charles Leadbeater proclaimed him a channel for the Buddha Maitreya—the future Buddha of friendliness. This designation implied that he would be a friend to humanity, reminding people of their innate Buddhahood and inner domain of self-knowledge and self-power.

This makes J. Krishnamurti especially relevant for dealing with life's difficult circumstances. Though he renounced his institutional role as "world teacher," he maintained an attitude of deep friendliness toward all of humanity during a time when the world was reeling from one crisis after another. He sought to guide people toward realizing their inner power and understanding. Krishnamurti's impact during rapid globalization, when the world was becoming a global village, and ideas from the East and West were merging, cannot be overemphasized. In many ways, he harkened back to the oldest truths of the Buddha himself.

J. Krishnamurti has said, "Be a light unto oneself." This closely echoes the Buddha's words: '*Aapo Deepo Bhava*' ('*Atta Dip Bhava*' *in Pali*)—Be a light unto yourself! In this one sutra or aphorism can be found the very seed of all self-knowledge and self-power because, as Krishnamurti says: "Self-knowledge is the beginning of wisdom, which is the ending of fear." Fear is the most abiding quality when we face tough times in our lives. If we eliminate fear at its roots, we are equipped to deal with all circumstances in life. Therefore, like the Buddha, Krishnamurti emphasized that self-knowing is the beginning of the wisdom that helps us transcend all fear and limiting circumstances.

Krishnamurti also states: "To understand yourself is the beginning of wisdom." Understanding this root enables us to navigate dark times. Moreover, we can become a "light unto the world" when it itself is undergoing dark times, as in the present age. Society begins to emerge from its morass only if individuals within it become more self-enlightened and realize the fount of self-knowledge and self-power within themselves.

Hence, Krishnamurti poignantly said: "You have to be a light to yourself in a world that is utterly becoming dark." In other words, there is no other way; the world faces numerous crises—natural, political, religious, and more. How do we deal with these changing times? How do we bring forth our dynamic abilities and find greater strength and power? It always returns to the same root: self-knowing.

As a child, Krishnamurti was very unassuming. However, one standout observation from his childhood was made by Charles Leadbeater, who discovered him walking on the beach by the Adyar River. Leadbeater remarked: "He had the most wonderful aura, without a particle of selfishness in it." This aura, this spiritual vibe in a simple and almost illiterate boy from South India, would one day inspire people worldwide to realize their inner treasure of being. Through knowing this inner treasure, one can shine amidst all of life's varying circumstances.

At school, Krishnamurti was considered dull and dim-witted. Yet, Charles Leadbeater was unwavering in his belief that Krishnamurti would significantly contribute to the evolution of individuals and all of humanity through his teachings of self-knowledge. Krishnamurti's acceptance of this potential made him akin to a vacant space—metaphorically called a 'flute' in the East. He was an 'instrument' through which the Greater could play its beautiful music and confer its profound message of genuine self-confidence.

True self-confidence—the ability to see oneself as having Buddha-nature and embodying the entirety of divine possibility—is the mystical root of dealing with difficult circumstances. It's not merely about hard work. Many believe that relentless striving is essential, but in the visions of the Buddhas and Krishnamurti, struggling without first seeking self-knowledge is pointless. Achieving self-knowledge brings wholeness, integrating one's innermost energies, and is the key to success in life. When energies are inwardly integrated and not fragmented, as Krishnamurti would say, one acts with inner integrity and extraordinary energy. This universal energy functions more deeply through such individuals, making it the key to truly successful living. Without this essential element, there is no true success.

Krishnamurti represents a radical breakthrough in the annals of spirituality. He embodies the highest possibility for people who live and function within the material world while seeking higher harmony in all aspects of life: physical, material, spiritual, and beyond. Physically, he believed in discipline, advocating for the harmonious functioning of mind and body. He often said that the best machine is the one that creates very little sound and very little friction. He emphasized refining oneself at the physical level—watching what one eats and drinks carefully. This was his only discipline: mindful consumption. If this first step is correct, one can move into the higher realm of intuitive wisdom—the spiritual realm.

Upon reaching the realm of intuitive wisdom, nothing can disturb you. No problem can penetrate this state of being.

Nothing can shatter you within because you can absorb much more than you ever believed possible. You become so full of energy, such a receptive being, that you can respond to all sorts of problems.

This may seem difficult, but it is the simplest thing to do in Krishnamurti's vision. It reflects the ancient Hindu philosophy of Sahaj Marg. Sahaj Marg is the path of spontaneous acceptance, the ability to absorb myriad problems without reacting to them with old patterns of anxiety, fear, and so on. There is no need to respond in such ways.

Respond with the understanding that you carry the nature of the Buddha within you. This imbues you with great self-confidence; where there is self-confidence, there is self-power. Nothing can break you because you develop infinite patience. You can relax even in the most anxious situations, maintaining composure in circumstances that would otherwise cause great concern. This is because you are finally living a total life, undisturbed by external happenings. Inwardly, you remain calm and meditative—a dynamic space that allows you to participate more meaningfully in the world. You respond restfully without creating inner tension or disturbance. Functioning from a place of non-tension, you can perform at your utmost, bringing forth your very best. Something within you starts working to a higher degree.

Ultimately, Krishnamurti's message helps us function to the highest degree of self-potential, shedding all negatives that hold us back. By chipping away at these negatives, you stand in the full might of your self-power. This is essential to self-knowledge. Krishnamurti's way was the way of negation. He spoke of eradicating superficial thought processes that prevent us from being our true selves.

In summary, Krishnamurti's teachings offer a path to self-knowledge and self-power. By understanding and integrating our inner energies, we can achieve true success and live a life of harmony and integrity. His message remains profoundly relevant in our rapidly changing world, urging us to become lights unto ourselves and, through that, lights unto the world.

Most of our thought processes are unnecessary; they are repetitive ideas filled with anxiety about what happened yesterday or what might happen tomorrow. When you free yourself from this cycle, you become aware of a greater power and freedom within yourself. This inner freedom allows you to tap into your highest reality. When you access this highest reality, nothing can stop you from creating the life you truly want.

Krishnamurti experienced some extremely tough times at a very young age. His life was like a roller coaster—one day in poverty, the next in opulence after being proclaimed the head of the Theosophical Order, the Order of the Star. Then came his complete disenchantment with the process, leading to his renunciation. Amid this turmoil was the death of his brother Nitya, which deeply affected him, breaking him mentally and psychologically.

Yet, this very 'breaking' allowed Krishnamurti to emerge evolved and strong, like iron forged in the hottest fires. The toughest moments and the lowest points in his life enabled Krishnamurti to become his most dynamic and powerful spiritual self. His life teaches us to move beyond our patterns of anxiety and feelings of hurt or being shattered by material and physical events. We must hearken back to the inner strength that is always ours, the legacy the universe wants to bestow upon us.

Be silent and receive that legacy. Understand that our only enemies are our inner enemies: anxiety, tension, and the feeling that we are less than a Buddha. Gautam Buddha used to say that all beings are Buddhas: some know it, while many do not. But recognizing this is the only way to stand tall. Know that you carry the seed of Buddhahood within yourself. Know that you have a Buddha-nature within! This understanding opens your mind and spiritual heart. You free your mind by realizing you are much greater than ever. You feel a profound transformation and inner liberation, allowing you to access your true potential. When you realize you are born with a mission and a purpose, you become life-affirmative.

During difficult times, people often become life-negative. A single negative incident can make them lose hope in life itself, causing them to over-worry about material aspects like physical well-being, work, finances, and relationships. Inevitably, things can go wrong in these areas, making us feel overwhelmed. However, when you recognize that within you lies a luminous body of light, what you may call the Buddha-energy, you awaken to your higher self.

Awakening to your higher self makes this energy available in everything you do. It is never far from you; it resides within you. This realization can lift you beyond misery, sorrow, and bitterness, allowing you to flow dynamically in whatever you do. When you flow dynamically, you truly attain virtue. This is the true virtue of the Buddhas: the ability to move forward and keep walking. As the Buddha said, "*Charaiveti, Charaiveti,*" just flow on through all circumstances.

Human beings are comprised of various layers of being. There is the gross layer of physical and material aspects, a deeper sphere of intellect, and the innermost sphere of our deepest consciousness. This innermost sphere is where you must look for power within yourself. The problem is we often refer to our material, physical, or mental selves for solutions, but our minds can create more anxiety. Thought alone can never resolve our existential problems. Real problems are addressed through the power of self-consciousness and self-knowing.

This inner light makes us aware of our true purpose and allows us to transcend difficulties.

By understanding and embracing this inner light, we find the strength to remain life-affirmative, even in the face of challenges. We become capable of moving beyond negativity and tapping into our highest potential. This journey of self-discovery and self-knowledge is the key to living a fulfilling and empowered life aligned with our true purpose.

It is often said that even a small amount of light can serve as a beacon along the path of life, dispelling darkness!

Light the lamp within yourself. Realize that you are a child of a wondrous universe endowed with a profound inner power. When you recognize this, you no longer feel small. Observe what happens to people facing tough times—they start feeling small and shrunken. This sense of being smaller than your problems is self-betrayal. You are always larger than your problems. The consciousness within you is divine in nature—far bigger, mightier, and more wondrous than any event in the physical or material realm. Remembering this is the beginning of self-knowledge and the key to facing life's challenges without stress, strain, or anxiety. This attitude allows you to be passive, relaxed, yet completely dynamic, creating a kinetic energy that effortlessly meets challenges.

It's a question of feeling enriched within your being. What does self-knowledge do? It brings you to the realization that "Yes, within myself, I am immensely endowed with treasure, power, and inward richness!" When you feel this inward richness, you can face outward challenges with greater confidence and a totality of mind and heart. This concept of totality is central to Krishnamurti's teachings. He frequently spoke of the totality of being. The totality of being must come from the very source of yourself, from the deepest aspect of your being. This is the art of self-knowledge. True catharsis comes from this pure, pristine, powerful space within yourself and the cleansing of anxieties, fears, and trepidations.

With this inner strength, you carry a great awareness and alert energy, ready to face any battle or challenge in life. This energy can burn down challenges through the fire of your inner knowing. Recognizing your inner light enables you to dispel darkness, meet challenges dynamically, and live with a profound sense of purpose and confidence.

Krishnamurti often spoke about the fire of self-knowledge, emphasizing its ability to burn away all that is negative within us. This metaphor of 'fire' is prevalent across many religions besides Buddhism. In Zoroastrianism, fire is central to worship. In ancient Hinduism, as reflected in the Vedas, fire symbolizes inner purity and the power to eliminate negative tendencies such as jealousy, anger, and other destructive emotions. Once these are eradicated, the ego dissolves, the limited self-vanishes, and our protective comfort zone is shattered. This process is akin to a caterpillar transforming into a butterfly—a rebirth that is the fruit of self-wisdom and self-knowledge. It allows you to delve into your deepest self and emerge like a phoenix from the flames. This phoenix, a symbol of divine energy, propels you into greater courage, bravery, wisdom, and enlightened action amidst challenges.

In essence, this transformation is what the Buddha taught.

This teaching also aligns with Krishna's profound wisdom in India's great spiritual text, the *Bhagavad Gita*. Krishnamurti was a pioneer in that he never relied on religious scriptures, yet he encapsulated their essence in a modern idiom. He avoided the jargon of ancient religions, presenting their core teachings in a contemporary form. These teachings advocate for a creative, dynamic, and fearless life. When you embody these qualities, nothing can stop you from achieving your fullest potential. True success stems from recognizing and harnessing the power within yourself.

Interestingly, the Western world's "pop genre" of "superheroes" echoes this spiritual metaphor. We must never negate the influence of mystical figures such as the Buddha on popular culture. Several aspects of Buddha-inspired figures, such as *Yoda* (from Star Wars), reflect the sagacity of mystical spirituality and cosmic awareness that the Buddha inspired people.

The immense popularity of superheroes in comic books and films stems from the ancient spiritual truth that the greatest power lies within us. We can achieve extraordinary feats if we realize and tap into this inner power. This genre resonates because it speaks to an inherent belief that, despite external circumstances, we have the capacity for greatness and transformation within us. Realizing this inner power is the first step toward living a fulfilled, fearless, and dynamic life. Krishnamurti's teachings remind us that self-knowledge is the beginning of wisdom, which leads to the end of fear. By embracing this wisdom, we can navigate life's challenges with confidence and strength, ultimately achieving true success and inner peace and realizing that inner power means nothing can stop us. This metaphor is simple yet profoundly relevant to the process of self-realization. Consider the popular tale of 'Batman': his source of courage resides deep within himself, symbolizing the inner power within Bruce Wayne. This applies to all superheroes. Even "Superman," with his superhuman abilities and consciousness, must navigate personal crises. He oscillates between the personas of Clark Kent and Superman. Still, ultimately, his spiritual search for a higher being within himself endows him with the nobility and virtue needed to act courageously in the world. Possessing superpowers alone doesn't bring real courage or wisdom; these come from internalizing and connecting with the greatest power within oneself. This process of internalization is at the heart of Krishnamurti's teachings.

Internalization is the crux of the archetypal hero that humanity has always revered. Whether in

Homer's Odyssey or India's Ramayana, the hero discovers a deep well of nobility, courage, and self-power. This discovery comes from self-knowledge and finding the light within, as J. Krishnamurti and Gautam Buddha emphasized.

In the Odyssey, King Odysseus embarks on a challenging voyage, facing numerous crises and tough circumstances, yet emerging victorious through his internal strength and wisdom. Similarly, in the Ramayana, Prince Ram overcomes all obstacles. It isn't just their skills as warriors that make Odysseus and Ram great; their internal qualities of spirit, courage, and calmness in the face of adversity truly define them.

Krishnamurti's emphasis on self-knowledge as the beginning of wisdom parallels these heroic journeys. He believed that understanding oneself allows one to navigate challenges gracefully and with strength. This internalization process, the act of looking within and finding one's own light, enables us to face difficulties without being overwhelmed.

Krishnamurti's teachings hold that this inner light and self-knowledge are not just for overcoming personal crises but also for achieving a higher state of being. This higher state involves living with dynamism, creativity, and fearlessness. True success and fulfillment come from realizing and harnessing this inner power. This is the essence of Krishnamurti's message: living a life rooted in self-awareness and inner strength enables us to face the world's challenges with a profound sense of peace and resilience.

Thus, the journey toward self-realization is not just about acquiring skills or overcoming external obstacles; it's about the inner journey of discovering and nurturing the light within. Once realized, this inner light becomes the source of true courage, wisdom, and dynamic living, allowing us to navigate life's adversities with grace and strength.

Indeed, we need to align with the innate spirit of our higher nature, allowing it to ignite our power within the material realm of life. By tapping into our own power of spirit, we unlock the true essence of living a remarkable human life—limitless and boundless. In the Ramayana, the tale of Hanuman illustrates this beautifully. When Hanuman faces self-doubt amid challenges, the reminder of his innate heroism by his comrades catalyzes him to reconnect with his inner power. Similarly, Krishnamurti acts as a mirror, guiding us to delve deep within ourselves and unearth our inherent strength.

Krishnamurti often likened himself to a mirror, reflecting our own greater power to us. As we embrace this power, we liberate ourselves from tensions, anxieties, and fears, stepping into a realm of positivity and strength. With this newfound empowerment, we become the ultimate warriors of our own lives, ready to face any battle that comes our way. In all mythologies, true greatness lies not in physical prowess but in self-power mastery—the spiritual treasure within. The attitude with which a warrior approaches the battlefield truly matters, transcending the outcomes of victory or defeat.

The Samurai of Japan understood this profound truth, emphasizing the importance of internalization before battle. They would delve deep into meditation, tapping into their inner reserve of self-power through self-knowing and meditative self-realization. For them, the battle was not just a physical challenge but a test of inner strength—an arena where victory was first achieved within the depths of the inner self. This inner victory paved the way for the manifestation of true warriorship on the battlefield.

Miyamoto Musashi, renowned as one of the greatest Samurai warriors and a revered figure in the Zen tradition, epitomizes the fusion of warriorship with self-realization. His seminal work, the 'Book of Five Rings' ('Go Rin No Sho'), elucidates the path of the fearless warrior attained through self-realization—a central tenet of Musashi's teachings. Similarly, Bruce Lee, a modern icon in martial arts, championed self-realization as the cornerstone of mastery in any discipline. Lee's deep admiration for J. Krishnamurti underscores the resonance between their philosophies, inspiring Lee's groundbreaking martial art philosophy, "*Jeet Kune Do*," which melded Krishnamurti's insights with Taoist and Buddhist principles.

The spiritual affinity between Bruce Lee and Krishnamurti underscores the significance of self-realization in navigating life's challenges. Though they never met, their convergence of paths is profound. Lee's emphasis on cultivating inward self-realization, imbued with grace, joy, and boundless energy, mirrors Krishnamurti's focus on aligning internal energies through self-knowledge. Both emphasized the innate power within—the Chi in Lee's terminology and the inner light in Krishnamurti's teachings—as the source of fearlessness in confronting life's adversities.

Jesus Christ, too, employed the metaphor of light to awaken courage within his followers. His apostles exemplified extraordinary courage in the face of adversity, guided by the inner light of realization. Their remarkable deeds, marked by unwavering faith and resilience, underscore the transformative power of self-realization to elevate ordinary individuals to greatness—a timeless lesson echoed across religious traditions.

Krishnamurti's revolutionary stance toward religious doctrines is unmistakable—he dismantles them entirely, urging us to look beyond belief systems and dogma. Yet, underlying his teachings is a profound acknowledgment of the universal energy coursing through us—a blueprint of divine potential waiting to be realized. This potential is tested in the crucible of life's challenges, beckoning us to actualize it.

Krishnamurti's language lacks religious terminology; he speaks of an indescribable energy, a force greater than us. There's no need for intermediaries—no masters—Krishnamurti asserts. Instead, he invites us to recognize him as a mirror reflecting our own latent capacities. Through self-realization, we unveil our potential for total attention, silent yet dynamic energy—a testament to human evolution at its zenith.

Krishnamurti suggests that human evolution is primarily internal—an unfolding of self-knowing that transcends external manifestations. Navigating life's challenges with grace and resilience requires cultivating this self-knowledge—a process of moment-to-moment discovery. As we tap into our inner spontaneity, uniqueness, and bliss, we unlock the boundless power of awareness within us. This limitless and boundaryless power emboldens us to confront problems fearlessly, emerging with solutions borne from profound understanding.

Krishnamurti implores us to become beacons of self-illumination—to embark on self-knowledge and enlightenment, blazing our own trails toward a life of unparalleled depth and authenticity.

CHAPTER 17

A List of Illumined Beings

To inspire individuals on their journey toward enlightenment, here is a list of significant Buddhist personalities throughout history. These figures embody the key teachings of Gautam Buddha and serve as powerful role models for spiritual liberation. Their lives and journeys toward enlightenment can be a valuable starting point for those seeking inspiration. Although Buddha emphasized the importance of finding one's own path and avoiding imitation, these enlightened beings offer guidance and insight to those on a spiritual quest.

INSPIRATIONAL PERSONALITIES

1. Yasodhara: Buddha's wife who, despite initially feeling abandoned when he left her and their newborn son to seek enlightenment, was later inspired by his teachings.

2. Suddhodana: Buddha's father, who became a disciple of sorts.

3. Rahula: Buddha's son, who became a famous disciple.

4. Amrapali: A courtesan who was deeply moved by Buddha's teachings, left her old way of life, and followed the path toward enlightenment.

5. Sariputta: One of Buddha's chief disciples.

6. Subhadda: A disciple.

7. Ananda: Buddha's beloved cousin and personal attendant, who attained enlightenment after Buddha's death

8. Angulimala: A former serial killer who attained enlightenment and completely

transformed his way of life after being influenced by Buddha's great mystic power and compassion.

9. Devadatta: Buddha's cousin who became jealous of him and attempted to kill him but was forgiven by Buddha.

10. Anuruddha: One of Buddha's chief disciples.

11. Mahakasyapa: A direct and important disciple, considered the first patriarch of Zen Buddhism.

12. Mahanama: Another chief disciple of Buddha.

13. Nanda: Buddha's half-brother.

14. Sundari (Sunita): Buddha's half-sister.

15. Vassakara: A disciple of Buddha.

16. Upali: A disciple of Buddha.

17. Bimbisara: King of Magadha and a great disciple of Buddha.

18. Ajatashatru: Son of Bimbisara and king of Magadha.

19. Anathapindika: A wealthy merchant who provided for many of the Sangha's events and stays.

20. Chunda: Siddhartha's uncle.

21. Jivaka: A wealthy person and disciple of Buddha.

22. Prasenjit (Pasinada): King of Kosala (Kaushal).
23. Visakha: A famous patron of Buddha from a noble family.
24. Shyamavati (Savati): Queen of Kaushambi.
25. Khujjuttara: A female disciple of Buddha.
26. Vajrapani: Said to have saved Buddha from an evil force.
27. Chunda Samanuddesa (Sunda Cama Putta): A smith who offered Buddha his last meal.
28. Nagarjuna: Legendary Buddhist philosopher, founder of the Madhyamaka school, and important figure in the Mahayana tradition.
29. Shantarakshita: A scholar who helped establish Buddhism in Tibet.
30. Shantideva: Author of the Bodhicharyavatara, a key text in the Mahayana tradition.
31. Silabhadra: A scholar and abbot of Nalanda University.
32. Luipa: A famous Mahasiddha from the Bengal and Odisha regions.
33. Tilopa: A renowned Mahamudra teacher who received transmissions from Nagarjuna and others and was the teacher of Naropa.
34. Naropa: The teacher of Marpa, who became a great Tibetan yogi and translator.

35. Buddhapalita: A scholar who expanded on the teachings of Nagarjuna.
36. Chandrakirti: A Buddhist philosopher who wrote commentaries on Nagarjuna's works.
37. Dharmakirti: A renowned logician and epistemologist.
38. Kamalashila: An author of important meditation texts.
39. Kumarajiva: A great translator and scholar from Central Asia.
40. Lilavajra: A tantric master and scholar.
41. Guru Padmasambhava (Guru Rinpoche): The great wizard and mystic master, who, along with Shantarakshita, helped establish Buddhism in Tibet and founded the Nyingma school.
42. Bhavaviveka: One of the founders of the Svatantrika school of Madhyamaka.
43. Bodhidharma: The first patriarch of Chinese Chan Buddhism, credited with bringing Buddhism to China and founding the Shaolin Monastery.
44. Bhadanta: Founded the Shaolin Monastery.
45. Buddhaghosha: A great commentator and scholar.

46. Gampopa: A student of Jetsun Milarepa and founder of the Karma Kagyu lineage of Tibetan Buddhism.

47. Rongton Sheja Kunrig: A renowned Tibetan scholar.

48. Taranatha: An important Tibetan historian and scholar.

49. Sakya Pandita: Founder of the Sakya lineage of Tibetan Buddhism.

50. Longchenpa: One of the great exponents of the Nyingma tradition.

51. Dolpopa Sherab Gyaltsen: Founder of the Jonang school of Tibetan Buddhism.

52. Machig Labdrön: A female student of Padmasambhava and a key figure in the Chöd lineage.

53. Marpa Lotsawa: The student of Naropa and teacher of Milarepa.

54. Milarepa: The great Tantric yogi of Tibet, known for his miraculous feats, mystic songs, and poems.

55. Karma Pakshi: The 2nd Karmapa and a key figure in the Karma Kagyu lineage.

56. Jamgön Kongtrül Lodrö Thayé: A polymath

and one of the most prominent Tibetan Buddhist masters of the 19th century.

57. Sakya Pandita Kunga Gyaltsen (Shakya Pandit): A great philosopher and one of the five founding fathers of the Sakya school.

58. Je Tsongkhapa: Founder of the Gelug school of Tibetan Buddhism, which is based on the Kadam tradition.

59. Yeshe Tsogyal: A consort and disciple of Padmasambhava and a key figure in the Nyingma tradition.

60. Atisha Dipamkara Shrijnana: A great Indian master who hailed from Bengal and was invited to Tibet, where he founded the Kadam school.

61. Sujata: The milkmaid who served Gautam Buddha a meal of rice milk the night before his enlightenment, helping him regain his strength for the final push toward realization.

62. Vasubandhu: Author of the Abhidharmakośa, an important text on Buddhist philosophy and psychology.

63. Garab Dorje: The founder of the Dzogchen tradition in Tibetan Buddhism.

64. Asanga: Founder of the Yogācāra school of Mahayana Buddhism.

65. Nagasena: A Buddhist sage who engaged in a famous dialogue with the Indo-Greek king Menander, as recorded in the Milinda Pañha.

66. Mahadharmaraksita: A Greek Buddhist master during the time of the Indo-Greek ruler Menander in the 2nd century BCE.

67. Dharmaraksita: A Greek Buddhist monk sent by Emperor Ashoka as a missionary in the 3rd century BCE.

68. Lokaksema: A monk from Gandhara who was one of the first translators of Mahayana scriptures into Chinese.

69. Zhi Qian: A monk and translator from Gandhara, who translated important texts into Chinese.

70. Kumārajīva: A Kushan monk and important translator of Buddhist texts into Chinese.

71. Dharmaraksa: An early translator of the Lotus Sutra into Chinese.

72. An Shigao: A Parthian monk and one of the first Buddhist missionaries to China.

73. Daoxuan: A Chinese Buddhist monk and scholar during the Tang Dynasty.

74. Huineng: The Sixth Patriarch of Chan Buddhism in China.

75. Faxian: A Chinese Buddhist monk, translator, and pilgrim who traveled to India in the early 5th century.

76. Dazu Huike: The Second Patriarch of Chan Buddhism in China.

77. Daoxin: The Fourth Patriarch of Chan Buddhism in China.

78. Guifeng Zongmi: A 9th-century Chinese monk who is considered the fifth patriarch of the Huayan school. He sought to reconcile Chan and Huayan teachings.

79. Yijing: A 7th-century Chinese Buddhist monk, pilgrim, and translator.

80. Zhaozhou Congshen: A 9th-century Chan master famous for his paradoxical and unconventional style of teaching.

81. Linji Yixuan: Founder of the Linji school, one of the five schools of Chan Buddhism.

82. Yuanwu Keqin: A 12th-century Chinese Chan master and compiler of the famous collection of koans, the Blue Cliff Record.

83. Xueting Fuyu: A 13th-century Chinese Chan master and abbot of the Shaolin Monastery.

84. Sengchan: The Third Patriarch of Chan Buddhism in China.

85. Bodhidharma: A 6th-century monk credited with bringing Chan Buddhism from India to China.He is considered the father of the martial arts (Shaolin), and I deeply revered in the Zen Buddhism of Japan as Daruma. In a way the entire way of the Bushido(The Way of the Samurai) traces back to Bodhidarma!

86. Mazu Daoyi: An 8th-century Chinese Chan master known for his emphasis on sudden enlightenment.

87. Ingen Ryūki: A 17th-century Chinese Chan monk who founded the Ōbaku school of Zen in Japan.

88. Wumen Huikai: A 13th-century Chinese Chan master, compiler of the famous collection of koans, the Wumen Guan.

89. Guoan Shiyuan: A 12th-century Chinese Chan master and patriarch of the Huanglong school.

90. Fazang: A 7th-century Chinese monk considered the third patriarch of the Huayan school.

91. Eisai: A 12th-century Japanese Buddhist monk who introduced Rinzai Zen to Japan.

92. Dōgen: The 13th-century founder of the Sōtō school of Zen in Japan.

93. Hakuin Ekaku: An 18th-century Japanese Zen master who revitalized the Rinzai school.

94. Hōnen: The 12th-century founder of the Jōdo-shū school of Pure Land Buddhism in Japan.

95. Kūkai: A 9th-century Japanese monk, civil servant, scholar, and artist who founded the Shingon school of Buddhism.

96. Shinjo Ito: Founder of the Shinnyo-en Buddhist organization.

97. Yamada Mumon (Gambo Yama Moto): A renowned 20th-century Zen master.

98. Shinran: 12th-13th century founder of the Jōdo Shinshū school of Pure Land Buddhism in Japan.

99. Takuan Sōhō: A 16th-17th century Zen master who taught the famous samurai Miyamoto Musashi.

100. Miyamoto Musashi: A 17th-century samurai, philosopher, and author of "The Book of Five Rings.". The greatest Samurai!

101. Hakuin Ekaku: An 18th-century Zen master who revitalized the Rinzai school in Japan.

102. Ryōkan Taigu: An 18th-19th century Zen monk and haiku poet.

103. Lanxi Daolong: A 13th-century Chinese monk who brought the Linji school of Chan Buddhism to Japan.

104. Nichiren: 13th-century Japanese Buddhist monk who founded the Nichiren school based on the Lotus Sutra.

105. Nichiren Shōnin: Another name for Nichiren.

106. Tsunesaburō Makiguchi: Founder of the Soka Gakkai, a lay Buddhist organization based on Nichiren Buddhism.

107. Wŏnhyo: A 7th-century Korean monk known for his commentaries on the Diamond Sutra and the Awakening of Faith.

108. Park Chung-bin: A 20th-century Korean Buddhist teacher and founder of the Won Buddhism movement.

109. Ŭisang: A 7th-century Korean monk who founded the Hwaeom school based on the Chinese Huayan tradition.

110. Jinul: A 12th-13th century Korean monk credited with founding modern Korean Seon (Zen) Buddhism.

111. Sitagu Sayadaw: A contemporary Burmese

Theravada Buddhist monk and founder of the Sitagu Buddhist Academies.

112. Mahasi Sayadaw: A 20th-century Burmese Theravada Buddhist monk and meditation teacher. He was a pioneer in spreading Vipassana techniques around the world.

113. Ledi Sayadaw: A 19th-20th century Burmese Theravada Buddhist monk known for his emphasis on Abhidhamma studies.

114. Taungpulu Sayadaw: A 20th-century Burmese Theravada Buddhist monk and founder of the Taungpulu Kaba-Aye Monastery.

115. Mingun Sayadaw: The first Burmese monk to hold the title of "Tipitakadhara Dhammabhandagarika," meaning "Bearer of the Tripitaka and Keeper of the Dhamma."

116. Pandit Narada: A 20th-century Burmese Theravada Buddhist monk who helped propagate Vipassana meditation.

117. Webu Sayadaw: Another 20th-century Burmese Theravada Buddhist monk who taught Vipassana meditation.

118. Mogok Sayadaw: A 20th-century Burmese Theravada Buddhist monk who popularized Vipassana meditation.

119. Sayadaw U Tejaniya: A contemporary Burmese Theravada Buddhist monk and Vipassana meditation teacher.

120. Shin Arahan: An 11th-12th century Burmese Theravada Buddhist monk who lived during the Pagan Kingdom period.

121. Sayadaw U Pandita: A 20th-century Burmese Theravada Buddhist monk and Vipassana meditation teacher.

122. Ashin Nyanissara: A contemporary Burmese Theravada Buddhist monk and the rector of the International Theravada Buddhist Missionary University.

123. Ashin Janakabhivamsa: A contemporary Burmese Theravada Buddhist monk known for his role in the Sixth Buddhist Council in Myanmar.

124. Sayadaw U Kundala: A 20th-century Burmese Theravada Buddhist monk who taught Vipassana meditation in the Ledi tradition.

125. Sayadaw U Kawi: A 20th-century Burmese Theravada Buddhist monk, scholar, and historian.

126. Sayadaw U Thuzana: A contemporary Burmese Theravada Buddhist monk known for his environmental and philanthropic activities.

127. Sayadaw U Pannavata: A contemporary Burmese Theravada Buddhist monk recognized for his missionary work in Sri Lanka and Malaysia.

128. S. N. Goenka: An Indian-born Burmese Vipassana meditation teacher who played a significant role in spreading Vipassana meditation worldwide.

129. Ven. Pomnyun Sunim: A South Korean Buddhist monk, author, and social activist known for his peace activism and humanitarian work.

130. Thích Quảng Đức: A Vietnamese Mahayana Buddhist monk who self-immolated in 1963 to protest against the persecution of Buddhists in South Vietnam.

131. Thích Nhất Hạnh: A Vietnamese Mahayana Buddhist monk, peace activist, and author known for his teachings on mindfulness and engaged Buddhism.

132. Somdet Phra Wannarat: A 19th-century Thai Buddhist monk who served as the preceptor and teacher of King Rama IV of Thailand.

133. Ajahn Sao Kantasīlo: A pioneering Thai Forest Tradition monk and teacher of Ajahn Mun Bhuridatta.

134. Luang Pu Waen Sucinno: A first-generation student of Ajahn Mun and a key figure in the Thai Forest Tradition.

135. Phra Khruba Srivichai: A 20th-century Thai Buddhist monk known for his temple-building initiatives and charismatic personality.

136. Ajahn Mun Bhuridatta The founder of the Thai Forest Tradition and teacher of many influential Thai Buddhist monks.

137. Somdet Phra Sangharaja Chao Kromma Luang Jinavajiralongkorn: The 18th Supreme Patriarch of Thailand.

138. Ajahn Chah Subhaddo: A highly respected teacher in the Thai Forest Tradition and a student of Ajahn Mun Bhuridatta.

139. Rahul Sankrityayan: An Indian polymath, known for his travels and scholarly work in Buddhism.

140. Anawrahta: King of the Pagan Kingdom who

reintroduced Theravada Buddhism to Burma and Sri Lanka in the 11th century.

141. Ashoka the Great: Emperor of the Maurya Dynasty who ruled from c. 268 to 232 BCE and played a crucial role in spreading Buddhism throughout Asia.

142. Harsha (Harshvardhan): An Indian emperor who converted to Buddhism and ruled from c. 606 to 648 CE.

143. Jayavarman VII: King of the Khmer Empire (present-day Cambodia) from 1181 to 1219, known for his patronage of Mahayana Buddhism.

144. Kublai Khan: The founder of the Yuan Dynasty in 13th-century China and a patron of Tibetan Buddhism.

145. Altan Khan: A 16th-century Mongol ruler who helped spread Tibetan Buddhism in Mongolia.

146. Bayinnaung: A 16th-century king of the Toungoo Dynasty in Burma who promoted and protected Theravada Buddhism.

147. Kanishka: A 2nd-century ruler of the Kushan Empire in the Indian subcontinent, known for his patronage of Buddhism.

148. Menander I: An Indo-Greek king who ruled in the 2nd century BCE and is featured in the Buddhist text Milinda Pañha.

149. Mindon Min: King of Burma in the 19th century and convener of the Fifth Buddhist Council.

150. Emperor Wu of Liang: The founding emperor of the Liang Dynasty in 6th-century China, known for his support of Buddhism.

151. King Mongkut: World-famous King of Thailand in the 19th century and founder of the Dhammayuttika Nikaya, a reformed sect of Thai Buddhism.

152. Prince Shōtoku: A 6th-7th century Japanese prince who promoted Buddhism in Japan.

153. Theodorus: An Indo-Greek governor and author of a Buddhist dedication in the 1st century BCE.

154. Wu Zetian: The only female emperor in Chinese history, who ruled in the 7th-8th centuries and patronized Buddhism.

155. Devanampiya Tissa: King of Anuradhapura, Sri Lanka, in the 3rd century BCE, during whose reign Buddhism was introduced to the island.

156. Udayin: The third emperor of the Haryanka Dynasty in ancient India, who ruled in the 5th century BCE and was a contemporary of the Buddha.

157. Dutugamunu: King of Anuradhapura, Sri Lanka, in the 2nd century BCE, known for his patronage of Buddhism.

158. Henry Steel Olcott: A 19th-century American civil war veteran who became a prominent figure in the revival of Buddhism in Sri Lanka.

159. Robert Thurman: An American Buddhist scholar, translator, and co-founder of Tibet House US.

160. Alan Watts: A British philosopher and writer who popularized Eastern philosophy, including Buddhism, in the West during the mid-20th century.

161. D.T. Suzuki: A Japanese scholar and philosopher who was instrumental in spreading Zen Buddhism to the West in the 20th century.

162. B. R. Ambedkar: An Indian jurist, economist, and social reformer who led a mass conversion to Buddhism in the 20th century.

163. The Dalai Lamas: The spiritual leaders of Tibetan Buddhism and, until the 1950s, the political leaders of Tibet.

164. The 16th Karmapa, Rangjung Rigpe Dorje: A prominent Tibetan Buddhist leader and the head of the Karma Kagyu school of Tibetan Buddhism in the second half of the 20th century.

165. Virupa: The Great Mahasiddha and Miraculous Yogi.

Be brisk in moving slowly!
Then, you will arrive soon!
Milarepa

I don't need anything. I don't seek anything.
I don't desire anything.
Milarepa

Exhibit true superiority by virtuous
conduct and exercise of reason.
Meditate deeply on the vanity of earthly
things and understand the fickleness of life.
Gautam Buddha

OM TARE TUTTARE TURE SOHA
OM MANI PADME HUM

Acknowledgments

I would like to express my sincere gratitude to the individuals who have played a pivotal role in bringing this series to life: Anuj Bahri, my exceptional literary agent at Red Ink; Gaurav Sabharwal and Shantanu Duttagupta, my outstanding publishers at Fingerprint! Publishing, along with their dedicated team. Special thanks to Shilpa Mohan, my editor for her invaluable contributions.

I would also like to extend my heartfelt appreciation to my parents, Anita and Captain Jeet Gupta, for their unwavering support throughout this journey. To my beloved sister, Priti and brother-in-law, Manish Goel, thank you for always being there for me. My niece, Vaanee and nephew, Kartikay, have been a constant source of joy and inspiration and I am grateful for their presence in my life.

I am truly humbled by the collective efforts and encouragement from all these remarkable individuals, without whom this series would not have been possible.

Pranay is a renowned mystic, captivating speaker and accomplished author who has dedicated his life to exploring the depths of spirituality. With a deep understanding of the human experience and an unwavering commitment to personal growth, Pranay has written numerous books that offer insights into the realms of spirituality.

One of Pranay's most celebrated contributions is his groundbreaking series of modules titled "Advanced Spirituality for Leadership and Success." His transformative PowerTalks and MysticTalks have garnered international recognition for their exceptional ability to inspire and empower individuals from all walks of life. Pranay's unique approach combines ancient wisdom with contemporary insights, providing a roadmap for achieving spiritual fulfillment while embracing leadership qualities that lead to remarkable success.

To learn more about Pranay and his transformative teachings, visit his official website at pranay.org.

To buy more books by the author scan the QR code given below.